Balancing Acts!

Juggling Love, Work, Family, and Recreation

Susan Schiffer Stautberg
and Marcia L. Worthing

To our husbands and sons, with love and gratitude for all they have taught and shared with us—laughter, joy, strength, and growth.

To our colleagues and employees who share the stresses of our multiple roles and are working with us to make the workplace more flexible and family-friendly.

Library of Congress Cataloging-in-Publication Data
Stautberg, Susan Schiffer.
  Balancing acts! : juggling love, work, family, and recreation/
Susan Schiffer Stautberg and Marcia L. Worthing.
    p. cm.
  ISBN 0-942361-37-7 (pbk.)
  1. Working mothers—United
States. 2. Work and family—United States. I. Worthing, Marcia L. II. Title.
HQ759.48.S74   1992
306.87—dc20   91-60815
                                                            CIP

Production services by Martin Cook Associates, Ltd.
Manufactured in the United States of America
Designed by Jacqueline Schuman

10 9 8 7 6 5 4 3 2 1

Contents

Acknowledgments

The conclusions reached in this book are based on empirical findings. Hundreds of men and women participated in Roper and Avon surveys—conducted by experts. In addition, we interviewed numerous women across the country. On a daily basis, both of our careers bring us into contact with women and men trying to balance their lives.

We want to thank the following people who participated in developing this book:

- The Avon representatives who took part in focus groups.
- Bickley Townsend for the Roper research and the introduction.
- Nancy Elcock for her excellent and thorough research and contributions to the structure of the book.
- Nancy Glaser and Gail Blanke for bringing us together in this project. Joanne Mazurki whose vision will expand the book's readers.
- Judith Moncrief Baldwin for time management advice.

Most of all, we extend our appreciation to the thousands of women who are out there balancing it all.

Preface

There is no question that today's women are busier than ever. Our families, our work, and our communities vie for our time and talents. Many of us are working outside the home, most of us are mothers, and a growing number of us are single mothers. How do we do it? How do we manage each day and its particular demands? That was the question that led to this book. Amazed at the varied and demanding lives of today's women, we began to think about a way to share problems and solutions. Every woman's work load is unique. At the same time, there is a great deal we can learn from each other.

Throughout our interviews with women, the theme that came up most frequently was "balance." "How do I balance my life?" "How can I find a way to blend the many responsibilities (and joys) of my life?" "Is there a way to feel less stress, less conflict over my many different obligations?" "Is there a way to do anything *besides* obligations and responsibilities?" "What happened to fun and leisure?" It seems that most women spend so much time juggling the many tasks in their lives that they rarely have time to sit back and smell the roses.

In talking with women, it is obvious that the most precious commodity of the '90s is time. As part of our research, we talked with several focus groups made up of Avon sales representatives. Here are a few typical comments these busy women made:

> I have so many things to do. I've got to be at work at 8:00 and I get off at 4:30 and after that I have to cook, take care of my daughter, and, at night before I go to bed, I check the books to see what Avon orders I have.

> You're so busy, you really don't have time for yourself; you just go with whatever you have to do—and do it!

There are so many demands on our time that it is difficult to take the time to think about what is actually most important to us. Too often, we find ourselves reacting instead of choosing. Throughout the book, you will see that we stress the need to know where your time goes. We think it is very important to establish goals in every aspect of your life in order to do the things that matter most to you.

Feeling a lack of time causes most women to feel tremendous stress in their lives. The biggest stress factors are conflicts between two or more desires or obligations. Almost every woman we talked to said that "trying to be two places at once" was the biggest source of stress in her life.

The women who best handle this stress are the ones who have learned to develop strategies for dealing with time demands in their daily lives. Some of the women use cordless telephones so they can cook and take clients' orders at the same time. Another jogs her delivery route in order to fit exercise into her busy life. However, the most common and successful strategy is setting priorities and staying focused. You'll see that a daily "to-do" list is the best friend of many very busy people.

Many women feel that there is little or no time for doing things other than responsibilities. Most women would like to find a way to be able to relax a little with their families, read a book, sit for a minute with nothing to do. They feel a need to be more involved with their communities, and would like to have some time to exercise. The problem is getting off the treadmill long enough to see a way to change the current imbalance in their lives and begin to include things they *want* rather than *have* to do.

There were common themes among the women we interviewed. Not surprisingly, the women who seemed happiest and most content with their lives were the women who had strong relationships with their husbands. There were husbands who did all the cooking, helped with the laundry, and were wonderful fathers. Unfortunately, this seemed to be the minority. Many women loved their husbands, but wished the men in their lives would do more work when it came to child care and housework. For these couples, communication was a weak point. They found it difficult to find time for nurturing their marriage when they were exhausted at the end of every day.

Another common theme among the women most comfortable with themselves was their dedication to taking some time for themselves. One woman described Saturday mornings as the time that she and her sister got together. Her family knew that this time was committed and that *nothing* could get in the way of this standing date. Other women mentioned bubble baths and the pleasure of trying different aroma oils. Their time in the bathroom gave them that window of daily relaxation and recharging so vital to their busy lives.

The third common theme among the happy women was their commitment to exercise programs. Whether it was "jogging deliveries" or swimming while the kids played, the energy level of women who exercised seemed higher than the energy level of those who didn't. The women who described themselves as out of balance frequently spoke of their need to lose weight and "get in shape."

It was clear that the women who felt best about their lives were those who had high self-esteem. This is natural because women's lives involve many daily decisions. The more secure a woman feels about her choices, the more likely she is to work efficiently. Those of us who question ourselves, look to others for all the answers, or undermine our own accomplishments are much more likely to get bogged down in daily life. We lose sight of the things that matter most to us, because we do not give ourselves the credit we deserve.

Those women who were hardest on themselves tended to sound alike. A frequent theme was that they just needed to be "more organized" in order to accomplish more. This is not as easy as it sounds because, while organization is a key to balance, it is also important to realize that our lives are frequently overburdened. If we continue to think that we can do everything, we will always be letting ourselves down. No one can do it all. No amount of organizing will help when there are too many things to do.

Underlying everything we say in this book is our belief in the power of the individual to change herself. No matter what past behavior has been, we believe every woman has the ability to take control of her life. It's important to remember that this is *your* life. If there are situations that are intolerable, it is up to you to change the way you live. You can't change anyone else, but you can change yourself.

Introduction

Two-earner married couples now outnumber couples with a sole-breadwinner husband by more than three to one (31 million vs. 9 million in 1989), and most dual-earner couples also have children under the age of 18 at home. But the fact that two-paycheck parenting has become the norm doesn't mean it's easy. In return for higher-than-average incomes, such families pay a price: an abundance of stress and a scarcity of time.

Indeed, as the generation who grew up expecting to "have it all" now struggles to do it all instead, it seems increasingly clear that something's got to give.

One possibility is that the "married, two earners, with children" segment will give up the struggle and revert to the traditional division of labor: Daddy earns the living while Mommy runs the home and brings up baby. This scenario seems unlikely, however, for several reasons. One is that both sexes *prefer* the dual-earner arrangement, according to the 1990 Virginia Slims Opinion Poll conducted by The Roper Organization. Asked which life-style would afford them the greatest personal satisfaction, a majority of both men and women today would opt for a marriage in which both spouses work outside the home and share responsibility for caring for the home and raising children.

The most stressed men are those with young children and a wife who is not employed. No wonder more men—with the exception of those over 50—would rather have a wife who works outside the home than one who does not. For men, shedding the sole family-breadwinner role has been a positive side effect of the women's movement.

Women, too, find satisfaction in employment; in fact, in identical proportions to men, they say that apart from the money they earn, they find personal satisfaction in the work they do. A majority of full-time working women today consider their work a career, rather than "just a job."

Still, women have become more ambivalent as they try to balance work and family. *Fewer* women today than in 1985—though still a majority—would opt for the two-paycheck marriage (53% vs. 57%). Fewer than in 1985, if they could do either, would choose to work outside the home rather than take care of a home and family full time. And women who are in the paid work force are less content to be there today—particularly if they have young children—whereas full-time homemakers are *more* content with their role than in 1985. Majorities of employed women with children under 13 agree that their job makes it more difficult to do things for their family, and that they feel guilty when they leave their child in the morning.

One critical factor fueling women's dissatisfaction is a gender gap in leisure time. Roper studies find that women on average report having an hour a day less free time than men (34 vs. 41 hours per week). Though both partners in two-earner couples have considerably less time than others, the gender gap persists, with employed wives reporting just 23 hours weekly of leisure time whereas their husbands have 31. These findings corroborate the qualitative research of Berkeley sociologist Arlie Hochschild, whose study of dual-earner couples, *The Second Shift,* indicated that many women return from a day in the paid work force to face another demanding work load at home. "These women spoke of sleep," says Professor Hochschild, "the way a starving man speaks of food."

Still, regardless of their discontent, perhaps the main reason most women are unlikely to drop out of the work force is that they can't afford to. Women today work primarily for the same reason as men: They need the money. Especially with the high housing prices of recent years, a large share of the "married, two earners, with children" group are making hefty mortgage payments that necessitate two incomes.

Another possible response to the work-family crunch is for couples to stop having babies. But that, too, seems unlikely. The baby boomlet, fueled throughout the 1980s by the bulge of baby-boom women in their 20s and 30s, is continuing, counter to Census Bureau projections and despite the fact that those women are now passing beyond their peak childbearing years. What the Bureau had not counted on was an apparent turnaround in family size preferences. Young adults today want more children than did their counterparts a dozen years ago, and evidently they are beginning to have them. Today's 18-to-29-year-olds, according to Roper surveys, plan to have 2.2 children on average—up from 1.9 for the same age group in 1977—and just 8% expect to remain childless, down sharply from 21% in the late 1970s.

If women are not about to leave work *en masse,* and couples are not going to forgo having children, where can we expect concessions to ease the work/family crunch? One place is at home. According to the Virginia Slims Opinion Poll, men agree with women that what would most help women balance their triple role as worker, wife, and mother would be more help from men with household responsibilities and child care. Yet women still do the majority of those tasks. As the 1990s advance, will men bring their behavior in line with their intentions, and step up their involvement in shopping, cooking, and child care?

The second place for such concessions is the workplace. Will employers adopt more flexible policies to ease the squeeze? Though "work and family policies" are receiving a lot of lip service, it was the business community that ultimately torpedoed the family leave bill vetoed by President Bush.

What happens in these two arenas will be critical to the long-term prospects for beleaguered working parents. Meanwhile, the busy two-income couple with children will need as much help as possible to balance their lives. *Balancing Acts!* provides the strategies needed to improve the quality of your life by seeking realistic goals that will nourish and help you take control of your life.

> —Bickley Townsend
> Vice President
> The Roper Organization, Inc.

What Is Balance?

Just what is "balance"? According to the dictionary, balance means many things. It is a noun, "a means of judging or deciding"; an adjective, "an aesthetically pleasing integration of elements"; and a verb, "to bring into harmony and proportion." It makes sense that this word has many meanings and nuances. We are complex and so are our lives.

How do men and women learn to have a life that beautifully combines, in harmony and proportion, their families and their work? How do they learn to both separate and combine the things that matter most? Look at that another way: How can we avoid feeling pulled in two different directions? How do we learn to balance so that neither job nor family seems to us to be shortchanged?

As Judy Mann, columnist for *The Washington Post,* says in the introduction to her book of collected essays, *Mann for All Seasons:* "We [women] find compromising between what we expect of ourselves as mothers and what we expect of ourselves as career women difficult. So we [have] juggled and balanced our lives—and lived our lives on the ragged edge of exhaustion." The question is, how can women juggle and balance and find harmony and proportion instead of ragged edges? Recent studies show that men feel this way too. They want to be more involved in raising their children. They also want rewarding careers and not just jobs and paychecks. As women's lives have become more complex, so have men's. Dual-career couples are trying to learn to juggle together in order to find harmony and balance.

Juggling

Juggling brings to mind those wonderfully talented masters of the circus who toss and catch all kinds of objects with ease. Whether they are launching hoops or lighted torches, their movements are confident and their grasps secure. The objects they hurl are in balance. Nothing comes too fast or at the same time. The timing between throws and catches is exact. Their performances are exactly timed with known standards of excellence. They are always in control and balance.

Too often, it seems we feel out of control as we juggle the diverse responsibilities and joys in our lives. Instead of smooth, seemingly effortless moves resulting in consistent patterns, women feel they are dropping objects as they lurch to try to catch every new item thrown their way. Remember that professional circus jugglers have practiced for many hours to perfect their patterns. In addition, these specialists do not have to contend with unexpected objects. Imagine the ringmaster telling the audience to throw out additional balls for the juggler to handle. Of course that never happens. Yet that's exactly what dual-career parents trying to juggle career and family deal with every day.

Think of the unexpected objects we are asked to add to our everyday juggling routines: a sick child, a pushed-up deadline, a broken toilet, an upset customer. These are all like additional balls being thrown to the circus juggler by the audience. And these calamities do not begin to account for all the possible disruptions in our lives. What about the unanticipated pleasures that might upset a schedule? How do we learn to balance the unexpected joys in our lives? What does a mother do when her child makes it to the city tennis finals? When a friend/lover/spouse has a wonderful job opportunity—in another city? What about free tickets to the *one* play or concert that matters? There are so many demands, expectations, and joys to handle. It's easy to see why working parents often feel stretched to the limit. How do they learn to handle anything other than the bare minimum? A job and a family are enough to test us. Naturally, we often feel on the ragged edge, but those edges can be smoothed over. Harmony and proportion are attainable. Balance can be achieved.

Individuals and families have different ways to achieve balance. There is no one absolute formula. Balance is not the same for everyone. What makes one person feel balanced may be another's roller coaster. Recognize that each of us uses individual ingredients for what gives us personal harmony and proportion. That requires us to be honest with ourselves about what matters most to us.

Setting Realistic Goals That Will Enrich Your Life

In order to achieve balance, we need to know what is important to us. Where do we want to go in our lives? What gives a sense of self-worth? The answers to these questions are our goals. Goals are targets to work toward. Goals give us focus and help us remember what it is we're trying to achieve with all the work that we are doing.

In learning to set goals, we can begin to shape the imbalances of our lives into a more cohesive and harmonious blend. The Chinese proverb that the longest journey begins with the first step is very applicable in goal setting. Experts recommend that we start with the large goals such as putting our children through college, staying married, assuming a higher position in the company. Look at where you are now in relation to that goal: My oldest child is seven; It's been two weeks since my husband and I have really talked; All the managers in my company have degrees and I don't. As we work to connect where we are now to where we want to go, we are helping ourself establish more goals. These intermediate goals are helping us break down a big task into smaller pieces. Already we are concentrating in a way that will help us use our resources more wisely.

As we begin to focus on our goals and break them down, we must be realistic. Ted Koppel was once asked if he'd like to be president of the United States. He replied that it was unimaginable as he was born in England and, therefore, it was constitutionally impossible. Ted Koppel is a realist. Realistic goals keep us on track.

As we break our goals into pieces we can also begin to establish a timetable. Elizabeth Jeffries, management consultant and author of *Person to Person,* recommends that long-range goals have timetables of five to ten years. She suggests that we break those down into intermediate goals that can be accomplished in six months and that our six-month goals be divided into tasks that can be accomplished in a week or a month. Achieving short-term goals helps maintain motivation as well as giving our work a further sense of value.

In addition to breaking our goals down, we should write them down. Writing our goals down helps commit them in our minds as well as strengthen their value. As each short-term and intermediate goal is accomplished, we should check it off on our master list. We must remember to revise our goals and appreciate that as our life changes, goals may need to be modified.

Another factor to remember as we set goals is that we are more likely to meet our goals if we think of them as benefits rather than tasks. Elizabeth Jeffries suggests that with every goal we ask ourselves "What's in it for me?" For example, if you wake up every morning and spend 20 minutes trying to figure out what to wear, your goal might be to organize your closet. Rather than just saying that your goal is to have a clean closet, you might instead think in terms of *giving* yourself 15 extra minutes every morning as a result of a neater closet. Those 15 minutes can then be used to meet another goal such as improving your health. Fifteen minutes a day can be used for exercise, a healthy breakfast, or devotions. Realize that the organized closet is a way of giving yourself another benefit.

It's also good to break our goal into sections that apply to the different aspects of our life. Each individual's sections will vary, but most of us can identify *career* goals, *personal* goals, and *relationship* goals. If goals are divided into sections it helps us see how we are balancing our life right now. If our personal goals are three pages long and our career goals barely make up a paragraph, we may want to examine our job and try to get a good understanding of why there is an apparent lack of opportunities and how that may·be affecting our work.

Do discuss your goals with others. Talk to your boss about your career path. How does she see your future, and what does she think about the importance of getting a higher degree? Tell your spouse that you want to be married to him in ten years. Part of setting realistic goals is figuring out what needs to be done to achieve the goal. By talking with others and sharing our goals we help ourselves focus on the specifics and we help ourselves stay realistic.

Strategies

Sharing goals with others and making a plan to achieve these goals is establishing your *strategy*, originally a military term; you could think of your strategy as your battle plan for balance. Perhaps a better term is "game plan." Every coach has an overall strategy on the way the team can best achieve victory. There is an overall strategy for the season as well as a specific strategy for each opponent. Bill Parcells, head coach of the 1991 Super Bowl champion New York Giants, developed a seasonal strategy around his team's running game and outstanding defense. In addition, he had to plan the best way to use this strategy, depending upon the particular strengths and weaknesses of the opposing team.

Individuals and families can adopt the same system. As you establish and discuss your goals, figure out the strategy that gives you the best chance of success. The more specific your goals, the easier it is to plan your strategy. Remember, just like the football coach, to take advantage of your given strengths. For example: You and your spouse decide that your marriage is off track; you are constantly quarreling over things that don't matter. What you know is that you can have great fun together. Your goal is to tap into what you enjoy about each other. Your plan is to spend more time together, alone. You decide you need two evenings a month (we said that *strategy = goal + plan*) in order to achieve your strategy. For many of us that plan immediately requires a baby-sitter. Since a standing date is usually easier to arrange than a last-minute search, is there a way to plan a sitter for every other Friday night? As you discuss your needs with your sitter (and your children, depending upon their ages), you are developing a team plan. It may be that a few Friday nights do not work for the sitter, but with an overall strategy in place, you can adjust to the peculiarities of a given week and substitute nights and still get the desired results.

Strategy involves more than one person. Strategy is a system that takes into account strengths, weaknesses, and contingencies. Strategy involves looking at a problem or solution from several angles, not just yours. Be creative as you develop your strategy. Creative problem-solving is fun. If your goal is important to you and the other people it affects and encompasses, it can be realized.

Taking Control of Your Life

Setting goals and developing strategies is a first step in taking control of your life. Control, among other things, means acting instead of reacting. It is deciding, based on individual requirements, what needs to be done. Instead of reacting to a barrage of items thrown by others, control is acting on a few objects that must be juggled in order to give each individual a sense of harmony and proportion.

The following quiz is adapted from the book *Taking Control of Your Life* by Gail Blanke and Kathleen Walas. It will help you see if you're in control as well as point out areas that might need work. Take it now, add up your score, and keep the results in mind as you read each chapter.

1. Think back to when you were in high school. Have your adolescent dreams been fulfilled, at least the ones that were realistic?

Yes _____ No _____

2. Have you had to compromise a lot over the years because people who were important to you—your parents, spouse—had different expectations of you?

Yes _____ No _____

3. Now that you are more or less past adolescence, do you still have dreams? Not about winning the lottery or scoring the winning touchdown, but dreams that can be fulfilled—such as taking college-level courses or starting your own business.

Yes _____ No _____

4. How busy are you? Do you find there are never enough hours in the day?

Yes _____ No _____

5. Are the things that keep you busy (if you are busy) pretty much the same day after day, season after season?

Yes _____ No _____

6. How do you feel when you wake up in the morning? With a song in your heart, or is it more likely to be bored resignation?

Yes, I'm bored _____ No, life is a joy _____

7. Your children are always learning something new. How about you? Do you have frequent new experiences, whether you're employed or not?

Yes _____ No _____

8. Do you have good times with your family? Do you go on trips? Play new games together? Enjoy group projects?

Yes _____ No _____

9. If you have a family, do you find that you usually have something of interest to say to them?

Yes _____ No _____

10. Do you frequently wonder what you are doing with your life?

Yes _____ No _____

11. Do you like your job? Are you enthusiastic about it?

Yes _____ No _____

12. Look at yourself in a full-length mirror. Do you like what you see?

Yes _____ No _____

13. Have there been significant changes in your appearance in the last five years? Have you gained or lost a lot of weight, for example?

Yes _____ No _____

14. Have you neglected your health? Forgotten about check-ups? Dentist?

Yes _____ No _____

15. Do you have three different wardrobes—depending on whether your latest diet was successful?

Yes _____ No _____

Give yourself a point for each matching answer:

1. No	6. Yes	11. No
2. Yes	7. No	12. No
3. No	8. No	13. Yes
4. No	9. No	14. Yes
5. Yes	10. Yes	15. Yes

Add up your points. The lower the number, the more you are in control of your life.

0–4   You are very much in control and need just minor adjustments.

5–10   You are somewhat in control. Check through the statements to find areas that need adjusting. Pick one to start working on immediately.

11–15   You need to take steps to get better overall control of your life. Establish priorities and set goals and strategies.

How in Control Are You?

A way to think about being in balance is to know whether one is in control of one's life. It is important at least to be in control of the factors that can be controlled. Like the successful juggler, being in control is knowing what you are doing and where you are going. Control is the difference between acting and reacting. It's deciding, based on individual goals, what needs to be done next as opposed to having our days revolve exclusively around the actions of others.

Few of us feel we are in control of our lives. At the least, most of us would like to feel that we can gain more control. Accepting that you *can* have more control is a start, but how do you learn to get it? Once again, writing things down makes them more meaningful. For example, suppose that you want to gain more control over your financial affairs. In order to achieve control over money, it is important to know where it comes from and where it goes. A budget enables you to write down what you think your financial situation currently is and to plan what you want it to be. Writing a budget down is only the beginning. It is worthless if you fail to reconcile the reality of spending and earning with what you thought it was. If your grocery allowance is $150 a week, and at the end of the month you add up the receipts and find that instead of spending $600 you actually spent $1,000, you know that you need to rethink your plan and/or your spending. But the important thing is that you are beginning to have control because you know where that money is going.

Why Control Is Harder for Women: Expectations and Desires

According to New York psychotherapist Dr. Natalia Zunino, women may have a particularly tough time in taking control of their lives. She explains that "Men traditionally believe that their success is due to their own skill and hard work. Women, on the other hand, think that their achievements are due to luck or other factors beyond their control." Therefore, a vital step in taking control of our lives is accepting that we are responsible for our successes. As you make your list of goals, it might be a good idea to make a list of things that you have accomplished. You did not get where you are because of luck. Your achievements at work and home are the result of your efforts.

The importance of recognizing and taking personal pride in accomplishments is addressed in *The Confidence Factor* by Judith Briles. Among other things, the book deals with factors that successful women feel are important in gaining and maintaining confidence. For Jay Marlin, the first female senior vice president with Dime Savings Bank of New York, the single most important factor in building her self-esteem was "seeing accomplishments in something I had started or that I had done—in seeing others view something that I had created or started. It is the major reinforcement that builds my own esteem and confidence." Once we begin to accept and be proud of our accomplishments, we are *taking control.*

There's an advertisement on television that advises "never let them see you sweat." While that may be great advice concerning our underarms, it's an attitude that may keep us from patting ourselves on the back for a job well done. It's also a dangerous mind-set in that it can prevent us from asking for and getting the help we need at work and at home. Are you afraid to let people know how hard you work? Do you know how to ask for help? Being in control does not mean that you have to do it all.

Things to Remember About Achieving Balance

Balance is learning to have a life that beautifully combines, in harmony and proportion, our families and our work.

Ways to Achieve Balance

- Set realistic long-term, intermediate, and short-term goals.
- Develop strategies to achieve each goal.
- Begin to take control of your life.

2

How Our Thinking Influences Our Balance

I have a friend who begins each day by standing in front of the mirror announcing, "I forgive you, kid." It's a sweet foolish nothing for moving on from yesterday's mistakes. After all, this is not a forced march—the point is to laugh along the way.

Diane Sawyer, ABC co-anchor

The Perfection Trap

Judy Mann frequently discusses being less judgmental about how others balance their lives. She also discusses being less judgmental about how we balance our own lives. Do you feel *guilty* for not being *perfect?* The italicized words are unfortunately the motivating adjectives for too many women. We think perfection is attainable and that anything less is not good enough; therefore, we feel guilty. Perfection is not attainable. By trying to be perfect, you may find yourself doing nothing at all.

The desire to be perfect is another way of setting unrealistic goals. Harriet Braker, Ph.D., the author of *The Type E Woman,* explains that the Type E Woman is one who expects too much of herself. She expects that she can be everything to everyone and as a result is frequently done in by her own unrealistic expectations. The number-one unrealistic expectation is that "I have to do things perfectly." The Type E Woman considers any mistake conclusive evidence that she's a failure. If a woman feels she's a failure, she also will probably feel guilty.

Braker suggests that we replace trying to be perfect with doing the best job that we can—*not* the best job that could possibly be done (perfect), but the best we can do on any given task at any given time. Just as one needs to set realistic goals, one needs to view the accomplishment of these goals with a realistic eye. It's a trap to think that anything short of perfection is failure.

Let's suppose that one of your goals is to be more involved in your first-grader's school. You sign up as room mother, responsible for coordinating a few small parties during the year such as at Christmas, Valentine's Day, and the end of the year. For the first party, you plan to bake and decorate cookies in the shapes of Christmas trees, bells, gingerbread men, etc. Unfortunately, two days before the party there's a crunch at work requiring overtime, making it impossible for you to bake anything—just getting to the party is going to require a huge effort. You end up buying plain cupcakes and forgetting decorations. You feel you've failed because the party was not as special as you wanted it to be. You're ready to drop the whole project, thinking that your child will be embarrassed forever by his/her less-than-perfect mom. Forget it! They ate their cupcakes, had fun, and think you're a nice lady for coming by and seeing their room. Don't give up something that is important to you just because you can't do it "perfectly."

Harriet Braker lists three things that are caused by the unrealistic expectation to be perfect. None of them is good. They are procrastination, chronic lateness, and extreme evaluation anxiety. We procrastinate, or put off doing things, in order to avoid making mistakes. As a result, we do nothing. Always being late is often the result of trying to be perfect, whether it's what we look like or the report that we keep polishing. Finally, if we cringe at criticism and hate to take suggestions, it's probably because we are trying to be perfect. Any criticism sends the Type E Woman into a tailspin. Rather than take the opportunity to learn from a negative experience, we lose a valuable opportunity by feeling guilty because we failed.

When to Accept,
When to Change

> Give us the grace to accept with serenity the things that cannot be changed, the courage to change the things that should be changed, and the wisdom to distinguish the one from the other.
>
> Reinhold Niebuhr, theologian

As one works on goals and control, it is important to keep the above meditation in mind. Sometimes it *is* difficult to know the difference between the things that we can change (the things over which we have control) and the things which we must accept (the things which we cannot change). A good place to begin is to accept that you can't change another person. If your boss is a screamer, accept the fact that this behavior was well in place before you entered the scene. If the behavior is intolerable to you, accept that you are going to have to change bosses or wait it out until there's a management change. In addition to accepting that you can't change the behavior, it's also important that you accept that you are *not* responsible for it. Screamers scream.

It can be very difficult to know and appreciate the range of opportunities for change within yourself. There are the inner and outer selves to consider. In today's world of beauty bombardment—plastic surgery, diets, exercise, tinted contact lenses, etc.—the possibilities of outward changes seem unlimited. In fact, there are few outward things that cannot be changed. However, it's more important to pay attention to the inner self.

The Inner Self

> . . . self deception remains the most difficult deception. The tricks that work on others count for nothing in that very well-lit back alley where

> one keeps assignations with oneself: no winning smiles will do here,
> no prettily drawn lists of good intentions.
>
> Joan Didion, "On Self Respect," *Vogue,* 1961

The phrase "that very well-lit back alley" is one of the best to be found in defining the inner self. How do we learn to know our "well-lit back alley" inner self, much less respect it? Dr. Melvin Kinder, author of *Smart Women, Foolish Choices,* has also written *Going Nowhere Fast,* which is subtitled "Step Off Life's Treadmills and Find Peace of Mind." In this excellent book, Dr. Kinder uses the term "imperfect self" in the same way that Joan Didion uses "very well-lit back alley." For both, the inner self is the guiding yardstick for contentment and happiness.

For Dr. Kinder, there are three steps involved in finding and tapping into our inner selves. He calls them *Confrontation, Integration,* and *Liberation.* Confrontation is being honest with ourselves. Confrontation is acknowledging, to ourselves, the person who we are, not the one we appear to be or the person who we want to think we are. It is difficult to find the courage to confront ourselves. According to Dr. Kinder, there are two primary reasons people avoid confrontation with the inner self. First, most of us hate to admit that anything is wrong. We want to deny that we are in pain, that things inside aren't as good as they may appear on the outside. Secondly, we are also frightened of the unknown and therefore prefer the comfort, miserable as it might be, of the familiar. Don't let these blocks stop you from finding the courage to confront yourself. Get to know your inner self.

Once you've begun the confrontation process, the joys of integration can begin. Once you know more about who you are, you know more about what you want. Dr. Kinder says this is when we can get in touch with parts of ourselves that we had forgotten. It might be as simple as remembering and reclaiming a hobby or, perhaps, something that we felt was no longer appropriate to our lives.

Cliff, 44, a vice president of a large public-relations firm, married, with one child in college and another finishing high school, was a success by any standards, yet he was unhappy. His unhappiness with himself was evident to others by his constant irritability and wide mood swings. When he sought help from Dr. Kinder, one of their discussions centered on hobbies. Cliff admitted that he played a lot of tennis, but that he rarely enjoyed it. He remembered that as a boy he had been fascinated by trains. He had spent many happy hours learning about trains and talking with others who shared his passion.

As Cliff grew up and took on the obligations of husband and parent he forgot about his love of trains. Unconsciously, he began to think that trains were no longer an appropriate hobby for one with family and executive responsibilities. With encouragement from his therapist, he renewed this early passion and joined a society of other people who shared his interests. He quit trying to do what he thought was appropriate for an adult and instead rediscovered a part of his inner self, resulting in a happier and more peaceful person.

Liberation comes from knowing and acting on who we are, not what we think others expect us to be. By accepting our real self, our goals become realistic, our desire for perfection is lessened, and we become less judgmental of ourselves. An added bonus is that we can also become less judgmental of others. Accepting the imperfect self also means taking responsibility for our own lives. There are no more "If only . . . ," or "If it hadn't been for. . . ." Ideally, the word "if" becomes extinct in the integrated inner self.

How a Happier Mind Makes a Healthier Body

Research is proving that the mind has a tremendous impact on our immune systems. How many of us have gotten sick after suffering a major loss? Dr. Steven Locke, a psychiatrist at Beth Israel Hospital in Boston, believes that the growing awareness in the medical community of the mind-body relationship is tantamount to the advent of surgery and the discovery of penicillin. This awareness of the mind-body relationship is important in both the prevention and the treatment of illness.

The mind-body interaction can affect our health in more ways than we might readily see. Many of us use cigarettes or alcohol to ease our feelings of anxiety. If, through getting in touch with our inner selves, we can decrease our anxieties, it follows that we can ease up on the physically harmful habits and addictions that can lead to disease. By gaining control we can perpetuate good health. Rather than being intimidated by the mind-body synergy ("If I'm sick, it must be my fault."), we should take heart and see that we can help control our health by controlling and balancing our lives.

Learning to Be an Optimist: Changing the Way You Think Can Change the Way You Feel

We all know the expression that an optimist sees a half glass of water as half full while the pessimist sees it as half empty. What we may not know is that optimism and pessimism are not genetic traits; rather, they are learned behavior in response to events in the early years of our lives. In addition, the way we think about what happens to us may well affect the way things will happen in the future.

Martin Seligman, Ph.D., has written a valuable book entitled *Learned Optimism*, in which he examines the roots of the way we think about events in our lives and discusses the ways in which we can learn to change our way of thinking. He explains that the very way we think about a problem, setback, or disappointment can either improve or worsen the situation. The thoughts we have about a particular event and *our role in the outcome* affect what we do next.

Dr. Seligman talks about our thought processes as ABCs. The negative event or disappointment is our *A*dversity. As we think about the adversity, we establish *B*eliefs about the event. Our beliefs then become *C*onsequences. Read the following paragraph and identify the ABCs.

A young woman was stood up by her date for a Friday-night baseball outing with her officemates. She was extremely embarrassed and felt that she must have done something wrong to cause this man to not show up. She knew that her friends from work must think of her as a failure with men. Over the weekend she got more upset, and by Monday morning she was sick with the flu and unable to go to work for a week.

What happened here? The *A* is the adversity of being stood up in the presence of colleagues. The *B* is the woman's belief that it was her fault. The *C*, or consequence, is that she became ill and didn't go to work for a week. The crucial step is *B*—the reasons that we give ourselves for a particular event. This woman's message to herself was very negative. It didn't occur to her to think that the man in question was at fault, whether by poor memory or by just being a jerk. And did her friends at work really care? They would take their lead from her. They would think of her as a failure with men only if she acted like a failure. Adding further to this woman's negative consequence was that she spent the weekend thinking about what happened, thereby strengthening her beliefs. Some of us like to think things and events over in our heads for hours or days. Dr. Seligman refers to these people as "ruminators." It's not necessarily a problem to be a ruminator, unless you are a *pessimistic* ruminator. It isn't difficult to see the negative outcome of spending a weekend thinking that it is your fault for being stood up and further compounding it by adding negative beliefs about what your associates must think. As a result of negative beliefs, this woman lost a week over an event that might have been resolved in 15 minutes.

The problem with negative thoughts is that we seem to accept them much more readily than we accept positive ones. There is no reason to give negative thoughts more value than positive ones. Neither is there a need to dwell or ruminate more on imagined failures than on real achievements. If the woman left standing at the baseball game had been able to talk back to her negative thoughts, she would have had a lot more fun at the game, an energetic weekend, and a healthy week at work.

It takes practice to change negative thought patterns, but once we accept the ABC formula and learn to challenge our pessimistic beliefs, we also learn that changing our outlook can change our lives. Take a minute and fill out an ABC for a recent negative event in your life. What was the Adversity? What Beliefs did you have as a result of the adversity? What were the Consequences? With practice you may begin to see that consequences are not just the result of adversity but rather the way we interpret that adversity.

Thoughts About Rumination
—for Women Only

There is evidence that women are more likely to think and ponder events than men. We've all had the experience of trying to talk to a man about an event in the past, whether at work or home. Most men have forgotten the event or at least tucked it away. Women, on the other hand, can recall what they were wearing, what time it was, and who said what. No one knows why women tend to be natural ponderers. Don't think about it. Just try to do less of it. If you must ponder events, ponder positive ones.

Another thought pattern that seems to be more common in women than men is what Dr. Harry Levinson of The Levinson Institute has called "magic thinking." This means that people tend to assume that any action that takes place around them involves them. For example: Mary is standing at the elevator when her boss comes tearing out of her office. She barely nods to her employee and doesn't speak to her during the elevator ride to the lobby. After the boss leaves, Mary thinks it is her fault that the boss was so curt. Mary is thinking, "What did I do wrong? Am I going to be fired? Why does she hate me?" What Mary doesn't know is that the boss was called away by a family emergency and wasn't thinking about anything but getting to her destination. Mary's negative imagining will undoubtedly sap her energy for the rest of the day.

Creative Visualization

Creative visualization takes advantage of our imagination to help us achieve what we want. Imagine what your goal looks like and concentrate on the image. A runner might picture breaking the tape as she crosses the finish line first. By focusing on the winning image, we strengthen our positive beliefs.

Concentrating on a positive image is not just for athletes. All of us can learn to bring our goals closer to reality by developing positive visualization. Many of us do it now even though we may never have thought of our actions as visualization. We all know or have at least heard of people who say they always knew what they wanted to do with their lives. Rather than think of these people as having received a blessing that the rest of us missed out on, we might think they developed their ability to see themselves as *being* something before the rest of us.

Once again, keep your goals realistic. It's important to know that you can achieve your goals. Think positively. If you create a picture of an organized desk, you are closer to being there. By seeing the image, you inspire yourself to work harder to achieve it. Thinking and doing are two different things, but learning to think optimistically or positively will certainly make it easier to find balance.

Things to Remember About Thinking and Balance

- No one is perfect. You will always let yourself down if you think in terms of perfection.
- Tap into your inner self to rediscover and explore what is important in your life.
- Thinking positively will improve your health and self-esteem.
- Be an optimist and don't engage in pessimistic rumination.

3

Why Time Is the Most Precious Commodity of the '90s

If you haven't got the time to do it right, when will you find the time to do it over?

Jeffrey J. Mayer

The most precious commodity of the '90s is time. Time for our work, time for our families, and time for ourselves. As we search for balance and what it means to each of us, we will find that our best ally is time. On the other hand, the lack of time can be our biggest stumbling block in achieving and having the life that we want.

We all know that time is an absolute. There are only 24 hours in a day, and no matter how much we try to beat the clock, save time, or buy time, there are still only 24 hours in a day. We are all smart enough to know that we can't change the number of hours in a day, so when we speak of needing and wanting more time, what do we mean? Do we want more time for work, for our families, for ourselves? Perhaps what we want is more control over the finite amount of time allowed each of us.

According to a recent Roper Organization poll, 41% of Americans feel that off-time is the most important thing in their lives. This is the first time since 1975 that the number-one priority is *not* work. Obviously, everyone has a slightly different definition of what off-time is, but for most of us it's time away from work, whether it be housework or career work. Off-time is the time when we actually can do nothing, or, perhaps even rarer to today's families, do something spontaneous. Off-time is the time when we can relax and recharge, improving our effectiveness in all aspects of our busy lives. Off-time is choice, and time for choices is a big part of balance.

Choice also means that each of us spends our free time in different ways. Men and women need time for their own interests. It's great if the whole family plays tennis, but chances are that each family member makes different choices. Remember that one person's work is another person's leisure. For example, shopping is relaxing and fun for some, while others find it produces high stress. Millions of fans follow baseball every year—one book on the subject is actually called *Why Time Begins on Opening Day*—but, on the other hand, there are many people who find baseball boring and unimaginative. So an evening at the ballpark is not everyone's dream of heaven, any more than a day at the mall is. Off-time is valuable time because it seems so hard to find. Throughout this chapter we will be discussing time and ways to find more off-time.

It seems paradoxical that the United States has long been a leader in the development of time-saving devices but our people seem to have less time than ever before. For the home, we have learned to depend on the availability of self-cleaning ovens, frost-free freezers, and microwave meals. At the office, it's hard to remember the days before overnight mail and fax machines. Yet, we all suffer from the need for more time. We know that the number of hours in a day hasn't changed. We know that there are many new wonderful machines that do save us time. Why, then, is the time crunch so apparent to us today? Why do most women respond to the question "What would make your life better?" by saying "more time"? What has changed is the amount of information in our lives. We all know that this is true, but few of us realize just how much more information we are asked to process in our everyday lives.

The Information Age

Here are a few facts that help us realize just how much information is in our lives. They are taken from *Breathing Space* by Jeff Davidson (MasterMedia).

> More new information has been produced in the last 30 years than in the previous 5,000.
>
> There are 7,000 scientific papers completed every day.
>
> A typical weekday edition of *The New York Times* contains more information than the average person in the 16th century would encounter in an entire lifetime.
>
> The amount of available information now doubles every five years. By the year 2000, the doubling time will be every 20 months.

These facts should make us feel better about our time crunch and perhaps help us focus on what we do with our time. In turn, the more we know about what we do with our time, the better our chances of finding ways to use our time most effectively, thereby allowing us to balance our time as we choose.

Think about how much time you spend every day trying to keep up with information. One-half of the jobs in America involve the processing or communicating of information. Brain power has replaced muscle power as our chief economic force. Staying current with occupational information has become a key element in our professional success. Most of us have experienced the frustration of carrying around a briefcase of articles which we plan to read at home, only to find that the time to read them never materializes. To lug the same papers back to the office the next morning is demoralizing because it reminds us what we didn't get done. Compounding the morning's frustration is the fact that the next issue of whatever you haven't read undoubtedly will be waiting on your desk. We need to recognize that one of our biggest time demands is just trying to keep up with information. Don't think you are the only one who feels bombarded by new facts and theories. We all do.

Procrastination

There is always a film clip on the late evening news on April 15th, showing hundreds of people at their local post offices mailing their tax returns. It's amusing unless you, too, are a procrastinator. If so, you know the repeated panics you place yourself in by putting things off. Many of us are procrastinators, and all of us have probably put off something at some time in our lives even though we knew it wouldn't go away. Why do we procrastinate, and what can we do about it? Even if this particular time problem doesn't affect you, you should read this section because you may be married to a procrastinator or work with one.

A procrastinator is someone who puts things off. People who are not procrastinators find it impossible to understand people who are. The things put off can be as varied as dental and medical checkups, paying bills, writing a report, or doing homework. Unfortunately, a serious procrastinator is also putting off her life. Procrastinators usually have elaborate excuses for why a job isn't finished. Sometimes they even seem to believe the wild tales they invent. At their worst, procrastinators turn their anger at themselves into resentment toward the "taskmaster."

In trying to understand why people procrastinate, it's important to remember that most of their reasons are not completely clear to them. Research has shown that most people have underlying emotional reasons for procrastinating. Most procrastinators view the put-off task as overwhelming. Rather than understanding that large tasks can be broken down, they allow themselves to be inundated by small details which hide the true task at hand. Procrastinators are notoriously slow on the jobs they view as unpleasant or that involve skills they are unsure about.

Procrastinators often fall prey to the perfection trap. In thinking that a job must be done perfectly, it seems overwhelming because perfection is an unreasonable expectation. Procrastinators tend to be very sensitive to criticism and would rather avoid a decision than be viewed as wrong. In order to avoid criticism, they make perfection their goal. Procrastinators need to learn to *do* things rather than *thinking* about perfection and worrying about criticism.

It is easy to see how the information age has probably increased the number of procrastinators. There are many tasks in our lives that require the gathering of data. As we've seen, gathering data can occupy 24 hours a day. If the data gatherer adds a desire to be perfect to the task at hand, he or she will feel legitimately overwhelmed. Luckily, the information age has also produced wonderful insight into procrastinators and there are many proven self-help practices that work.

Establishing Momentum— Helpful Hints for Procrastinators

1. Admit that you procrastinate. It's much easier to solve a problem once it's identified. If you can, figure out what makes it hard for you to get started or maintain momentum. Do you hate to be criticized? Are you trying to be perfect?

2. Face the facts and then do something *right away* to tackle the task. Accept that putting a job off will not make it go away. In the case of medical checkups, delay could jeopardize your health. Call for those appointments now.

3. Break down seemingly overwhelming tasks into smaller pieces. If a 20-page report is due in two weeks, it can be divided into two pages a day. To help further, after your two pages are completed, make notes on what you'll be covering the next day. Getting started again is much easier when the task is defined. If your garage is a mess and you spend an hour looking for the battery cables, try tackling power tools one day, automotive accessories the next, and so on.

4. Ask for help. This seems so simple, but procrastinators rarely

ask for assistance. "Invite" your kids to clean out their old toys from the garage. If it is appropriate, appeal to a colleague for her ideas on your report.

5. Can the job be delegated? If so, do it. If you hate to do taxes, hire an accountant. The fee is much less than penalties.

6. Reward yourself for every task that is completed on time. It can be as simple as a bunch of flowers or a new book. Congratulate yourself and enjoy the freedom that comes from not being under the gun.

7. If possible, share with a friend your difficulty in getting things done. Ask for her encouragement and share your accomplishments. Positive reinforcement is the best way to gain and maintain momentum.

Once you begin to address the tasks that you've been putting off, you'll find that a natural momentum begins. As you rid yourself of unnecessary fears of criticism and unrealistic desires for perfection, your life will become freer. All the time that was previously taken up by worrying about not getting things done is now available for enjoyment.

A final thought on procrastination: Most of us have procrastinated during some period of our lives. Those who best conquer procrastination have accepted that they will not be perfect and that they will make mistakes. We can help reinforce this message to ourselves by passing it on to our children. Encourage your children to take deadlines seriously. At the same time, don't be unduly strict or judgmental when they make mistakes. Your children are as incapable of perfection as you are. You can encourage them to develop good study habits and be there to offer encouragement and suggestions when their tasks seem overwhelming.

The Key to Free Time
Is Organization

Setting priorities, planning time, delegating jobs, and saying goodbye to procrastination are all part of being organized. The best way to guarantee free time is to streamline as many of the responsibilities in your life as possible. Organization is not something available only to a few of us. Anyone can learn to be more organized. Being organized does not mean saying good-bye to creativity. It does not mean that you are a neat freak or an obsessive personality. It means that you value your time. It means an end to wasting time looking for things, doing things more than once, being constantly in motion with nothing to show for it.

Being organized enables you to have more discretionary time. Discretionary time is off-time, leisure time, free time, time to do whatever you want to do. The problem is, many of us feel we don't have time to stop and get organized. We are so busy we just don't have the time to stop and take stock. Make the time. At the office, start with your desk. At home, make a schedule covering every closet, drawer, and cabinet.

Organizing your home may be a bigger job, but the opportunity for help exists. Enlist your partner and children in a thorough cleaning out of all nooks and crannies. Think about opening closet doors in your house without having to put your arms up in defense of falling objects. Imagine your children finding the soccer ball without having to fumble through half their toys. Have a yard sale and promise the kids that if they help they will share in the profits.

Visualize a clean desk, files in order and labeled. Imagine your boss asking for last year's personnel report and instead of frantically fumbling for it, being able to open one drawer and pull it out immediately. It isn't hard to realize that you will save time twice if you are organized. The first time saving comes by finding what you want immediately. The second comes from not having to clean up the mess you made while looking.

Now that the desire to "get organized" is there, how do you accomplish it? As the principles of organization are the same for home and office, it's a matter of applying the principles to your specific problems. Know what is on your desk or in your closet. By going through every item in a given area, you will find much that can be discarded. Coupons expire, parties are over, conventions have ended. You may lose ten pounds this spring, but if you do, do you really think you'll want to wear that jacket again? Things that can be discarded should be thrown away immediately. (Clothes can be put in a bag and taken to a charity or thrift shop—just do it.) Everything else, whether a piece of paper or a shirt with a missing button, should be set aside, indicating it needs further action.

Once you've separated the things that need to be done, you are ready to bundle them into like groups. Put those things requiring a phone call together, those things requiring a written response in another group. At home, put all items requiring mending in one group. The key to dealing with your bundles is to *do* them. Stacks of items are no good. Once you've made the calls, answered the letters, repaired the clothes, put them away and out of sight. Throw away as much as possible.

Besides inventory, the other key to organization is to keep a current list of things that need to be done. Many people keep a pad in the kitchen to note needed items. When you see the cooking oil getting low, put it on the list. The advantages of a to-do list at work also apply at home. If you know what you want to get done, you have a jump on the next day. Rather than feeling overwhelmed, you have given yourself direction. As you accomplish your tasks, cross off the items from the list. Transfer any remaining items to the next day's list. Reevaluate each task as you write it down. Does it really need to be done? Omit whenever possible.

It doesn't matter if you live with a file box clutched in your arms, have all your lists coordinated by computer, or use the reliable legal pad. Use what works for you. If your handwriting is large, you may be more comfortable with lined paper than the small spaces in most organizers. There is no one system; there are only the tried-and-true principles explained here. The next chapter discusses a few time-management systems in detail. Remember, the goal is more time to do what you want.

Things to Remember About
Having More Off-time

- The most precious commodity of the '90s is time.
- There are *never* more than 24 hours in a day.
- Balancing time means making choices about what is most important.
- Procrastination can be conquered. You can establish momentum and learn to meet deadlines.
- Organization is one of the best ways to control your time.

4

Time-Management Tools

Time-management tools are probably the best way to find more time for what you want to do. Many of these lessons come from top management executives, but you will see that their models can be applied with great results in or out of the office. Not many of us want to be time gurus carrying file organizers, but most of us would like to find more off-time. Think critically as you read through these experts' tips and find the ones that will work for you.

Establishing Priorities and Saying No

Top executives interviewed by *Fortune Magazine* say that there are two keys to managing their busy schedules. The first is setting priorities, the second is saying no. Neither is easy, but both practices are crucial if you are to be an effective manager of time.

Whether you realize it or not, you are establishing priorities and saying no in your life now. The things you are getting done are your priorities and the things you are not getting done are the things you are saying no to. Think for a minute. Did you really want to have a summer vacation last year, but scheduling just didn't allow for it?

When did you schedule it, in January or June? Was it really a priority? The key in time management is to *know* that you are doing what is important. And the key to saying no is that you are saying no to what is not important. Effective and talented managers make establishing priorities and saying no *active* decisions.

The Pareto Principle, aka the 80/20 Rule

The Pareto principle, named for 19th-century Italian economist Vilfredo Pareto, is also known as the 80/20 rule. The rule states that 80% of the value of a group of items is often found in 20% of the items. For example, 80% of the food sold in a restaurant usually comes from 20% of the items on the menu. Eighty percent of all motion-picture revenues is from 20% of the movies released. Once you think about this rule, you will see that it has many applications, including setting priorities.

Start by making a list of what needs to be done. Look at it carefully and decide which things are most important. Put your list in order with the most important things first. Most executives find it best to end a day at the office by making the next day's list. Your mind is concentrating on work and it gives an immediate focus to the next day. When you arrive at work the next morning, you won't waste any time trying to get started. Instead, you'll be able to focus on that day's list. The 80/20 principle says that out of a list of ten things, if you only do the first two, you will have accomplished 80% of what was most important for the day. If there are things on the bottom of the list that keep appearing each day, but never get done, it may be that they should be taken off the list. They fall into the "no" category.

For me (Susan), the answer is a daily to-do list. Before leaving the office, I gather up the notes on my desk, and begin my list for the next day. At home, I add other items to the list as they come up. First thing in the morning I circle the "must do's" and get to work. I use a white pad that can fit in a binder. It travels with me everywhere.

Annual Calendars
for Work and Home

In addition to a daily list of things to do, the best managers agree that planning their time and setting their priorities includes keeping an annual calendar. Many executives plan up to a year and a half in advance, depending upon their particular business. Spread your year in front of you and enter important dates and events. These might include school meetings, important business engagements, community events, vacations, and birthdays. Depending upon the flexibility of the event, you might schedule in pen or pencil. Board meetings, for example, should be in pen as they are vital. A community event might be in pencil because it's optional. Many managers also find it helpful to use a particular color ink to indicate that a project might be delegated to a husband, a child, or a co-worker.

As you begin planning your calendar, it's important to keep it up to date and to share it with others. Talk it over with your spouse and your children. Set aside some time for each of you to compare your individual work schedules and enter the family demands. Vacations need to be planned together. Most schools, churches, and athletic leagues send out calendars. Use these calendars in planning yours. As you and your spouse compare notes, you may be able to pinpoint potential conflicts and solve them before they become major problems. If you have a job requiring travel, it's important to know when parents' day at school is before you finalize your out-of-town trips. Not all conflicts can be avoided, but with both parents planning, it is possible to minimize problem days and weeks. If you have a secretary or assistant, make sure she is working with you to keep the calendar accurate.

A great new time-management tool has recently come onto the market from FlexAddress® Systems (800-996-9886). Unlike standard looseleaf personal organizers, the address, calendar, and note pages are made of peel-off label stock. This means you don't have to face the time-consuming task of rewriting your address book, as individual entries can simply be stripped off, discarded, and replaced. Going to an unfamiliar place for lunch, dinner, or an appointment and don't want to take your organizer along? Just peel off that day's calendar entry, take it with you, and return it to your book later to complete your permanent record.

Saying No

Why is learning to say no so important? If you think about it, it's the easiest way to control your time. It's so easy to become overcommitted by refusing to say no. By cutting back on your commitments, you are able to be more effective. Fewer commitments, especially the seemingly small ones, give you a chance to work harder on the things that matter most.

Most of us find saying no difficult because we want to be liked and we fear that by saying no, we will lose some of our popularity. We also say yes too often because it gives us a momentary feeling of power or it's a way to avoid a conflict or confrontation. The situations arise daily. For example: A representative from the Parent Teacher group at your children's school calls to ask you to make 20 phone calls asking for volunteers for the school fair; your sister-in-law calls to invite you for Sunday dinner the one day you planned to do nothing; or an acquaintance is in town and wants to have lunch.

As you work to increase your ability to say no, keep the following guidelines in mind.

1. Say no immediately before people can anticipate that you may say yes. Answers such as "I don't know" or "Let me think about it" only get people's hopes up. A delayed no increases the chances of animosity.

2. Realize that you have a right to say no. You don't have to offer a reason every time you turn down someone's request.

3. Offer your refusals politely and pleasantly. There's no need to be defensive—it's your right to say no.

4. Offer a counterproposal if you think it's appropriate and the request is a valid one. "I can't sit in for you at the meeting this afternoon, Joe, but I'll answer your telephone while you are out."

Once you learn to say no, you will see that the tasks that you agree to do will be done more effectively as a result of fewer commitments. If you can learn to combine setting priorities with an increased ability and willingness to say no, you will find that the quality of your work will improve. You will be working harder on fewer things and concentrating your energies. Your time will be less splintered because you more often will say no to tasks that you don't need to be doing. As a helpful guide, it's a good idea to keep the following *not-to-do* list handy. If you find yourself slipping and know that you are working hard yet accomplishing little, check this reminder sheet to help get yourself back in control.

The Not-To-Do List

1. All low-priority items—unless the high-priority items have been completed.
2. Any task whose completion is of little or no consequence. When you have something to do, ask yourself what would be the worst thing that could happen if you didn't do it. If the answer isn't too bad, then don't do it.
3. Anything that you can give to someone else to do.
4. Anything you would be doing just to please others because you fear they'll not think well of you.
5. Thoughtless or inappropriate requests for your time and effort.
6. Anything others should be doing for themselves. This is especially true of children. Are they really unable to clean up their own rooms?

The Secret to Finding
More Time—Delegation

Every person has felt the frustration of having a million things to do and no time to do them. You've established your goals, prioritized your day, and planned your year, but you still feel that you need extra hours in the day in order to get things done. The next step in efficient management is delegation. Delegation is the tool that allows managers to free up time in their days to get the big jobs done.

As we have seen, frequently we fail to get things done because we may be overwhelmed by the task. There is just not time to get the job done. If we can learn to break down the big job into smaller segments, we can then take advantage of a key management tool—delegation. To delegate means to pass on the responsibility for a specific task to someone else. More exactly, it means passing on the responsibility of *doing* the task to someone else. As a big job is broken down into smaller segments, it is easier to distribute the work load. The overall job is still your responsibility, but the doing of the job can be shared.

If Delegation Is Such a Great Thing, Why Don't We Do It More?

Many people are reluctant to delegate. On the surface, this may be hard to understand. Why would anyone refuse the opportunity to ease their burden, and get more work done in less time? There is no more efficient way to find more time for yourself than to be willing to delegate, yet it is a management tool used well by too few. It is important to realize that *it isn't easy to delegate*. Some common reasons for failing to delegate are:

1. *Not wanting to lose control of a project.* A good delegator doesn't lose control. By dividing a project and assigning the various aspects of the job, a person actually has a better understanding of the undertaking than if the job had been taken on single-handedly.

2. *Fear that authority will be resented.* Too many people are held back by their desire to be popular. They worry that by delegating work they will be resented by colleagues. People who work hard and manage fairly are not resented. On the other hand, people for whom popularity, as opposed to respect, among colleagues is their first priority have trouble with this concept.

3. *Not trusting other people—you've been let down before.*

If earlier attempts to delegate have resulted in confusion and missed deadlines, some people may be reluctant to try again. They know that if they do the job, it will be done exactly to their specifications. This is both a lonely and time-consuming philosophy. Besides the potential value of new ideas, delegating increases the strength of the whole group.

4. *Fear of being outclassed.* This is a hard one to admit but much more common than most people realize. In business, some managers worry that a junior team member may outshine the boss. Instead of being threatened by a talented underling, pat yourself on the back for recognizing the talent within your own group. A key management skill is tapping into the talent of the people around you.

5. *Hating to give up your favorite part of the job.* A talented sales manager probably started out as a crackerjack salesperson. Many people hate to leave the comfort of the part of the job that they know is their strength. Remember that advancement means change, not remaining stuck in the old job duties.

What to Delegate

It's important to remember that the purpose of delegation is to free up time. How do you decide which tasks are the best for you to delegate? In their book *Don't Do. Delegate!,* James Jenks and John Kelly suggest that tasks that fit the following criteria are often most suitable for delegation:

1. *Routine.* You know the task well and therefore can be a strong supervisor. In addition, because the task is routine you are setting up a system that will free time every week.

2. *Necessity.* These are the jobs that must be done but don't necessarily require judgment or discretion.

3. *Trivia.* Trivia, like beauty, is in the eye of the beholder. If you are in charge of plant maintenance you needn't supervise every air-conditioning repair, but you probably want to keep a close eye on the elevator inspections.

4. *Specialties*.   No one, especially in the information age, can be an expert on everything. Know when to hire outside help or tap into the specific talent within your company.

5. *Chores*.   Think of chores as tasks that you do not like to do or things that you are sick of doing.

6. *Pet Projects*.   Think of a salesman who couldn't give up the route even though it was no longer the best use of managerial time. Look carefully at your favorite things and see if perhaps some of them can't be delegated. Your own enthusiasm will be a great motivator for your successor.

Saving Time at Home

The same techniques for freeing up time at the office can be applied to the home. There is one difference, and it's a good one. You and your spouse are now the Chairman and CEO. The decisions as to what to spend time on are all yours. That sounds simple, but many of us are not taking advantage of our authority. We have failed to adjust our expenditures of time at home to take into account the many additional pressures of our lives outside the home.

We've all arrived home and instead of relaxing and talking to our husbands and children, we've changed clothes and plunged into our second career. In the majority of U.S. families, both partners have full-time jobs. In many others, there is only one full-time parent and that parent also holds down a full-time job. With parents coming home from work and facing yet another set of demands, it's no wonder that off-time seems a dream. How many of your weekends are taken up by laundry, cleaning house, or other *tasks* that you feel need to be done in order to be happy with the way your home operates? By applying the same time-management techniques in the home that work so well in the office, off-time can become a reality. Co-partners should look at their life away from the office and see if they have established priorities, learned to say no, and taken advantage of delegation.

What Do You and
Your Partner Want?

Again, it's the simplest questions that we fail to ask. How many of you have spent time with your partner making a list of what really matters to you regarding your home life and how you can accomplish it? The "how" are we going to achieve this is much harder than the "what"—it's your strategy for your home. You know your house runs more efficiently if the laundry doesn't pile up, but can you figure out how and when the laundry can be done? We would all like to eliminate trips to the grocery store, but who takes the responsibility for the grocery list and shopping? If partners can work together at home the same way they do with colleagues at the office —making to-do lists, establishing priorities, assigning responsibilities—they will find a lot more time to be spontaneous and have a lot more fun.

How Clean Is Clean?
Does Neatness Count?

Many of us were brought up in homes where mothers didn't work full time outside the home. Therefore, the house sparkled and there was a hot meal on the table every night. In the last 20 years, more and more women have been working outside the home. Many of them have also tried to maintain their mothers' quality of housekeeping. Because many women and men have traditionally undervalued housework, no one really took into account how much time it takes to keep a house clean and running smoothly. With the advent of time-saving products for the home such as dishwashers and permanent-press clothing, experts were warning of the problems of too much leisure time. Those problems never materialized. Only now are men and women recognizing that housekeeping is both important to a family and very time-consuming. Why does housekeeping take so much time, and why isn't it more rewarding?

The biggest problem with housekeeping is that it involves doing the same tasks over and over. Making beds, cleaning stove tops, washing dishes, and sweeping up pet hair are all repetitive tasks. While it can be rewarding to know that your house is clean from top to bottom, that reward can become less valuable as you realize that you have to repeat the same tasks every day (sometimes more than once a day) in order just to keep up. Housework is never done. There is no higher plateau to strive for. It is easy to become a slave to housework, especially if you are convinced that every other house on your street is spotless and it is only your house that fails the white-glove test. Relax. You and your partner are the only ones who need to be satisfied. Remember the 80/20 rule. Eighty percent of the necessary work is in 20% of the tasks.

Delegating Home Chores or Getting Someone Else to Do Them

There is virtually no service that isn't for sale in today's society. People will walk your dogs, organize your closets, buy your clothes, handle the choosing as well as wrapping and mailing of all gifts, and stand in line for you. Are there areas of your life that could benefit from some expert help? Because these services are specialized, many are more efficient than we might be ourselves. It's hard to be a renaissance man or woman in today's world. Besides saving time, you will often be saving money.

Routine tasks at home, like those in the office, can often be assigned to outside help.

1. A cleaning service or helper once a week will keep dirt under control.
2. Take advantage of the many "package" services available. They are frequently more efficient than spending time in long post-office lines or trying to get to the nearest U.P.S. drop-off center.
3. Catalog shopping and toll-free numbers are also time savers. A telephone call can handle everything from gardening supplies to furniture. (One way for busy women to save time—and money—is to shop through Avon. You can pick and choose

either at home or at your place of work—on your schedule. It's also possible to return or exchange anything you buy. There's even an 800 number to call if you don't have an Avon representative: 800-858-8000).

4. Eating is something we do three times a day. Someone has to cook what we eat. Even those of us who like to cook usually don't want to cook three meals a day, every day. The stores are full of microwave meals, some more nutritious than others. Take-out and delivery services abound. Find the good ones in your area and keep the menus handy.

Organizing Tasks in Bundles

Now that some of the routine chores have been delegated, look at what is left over and plan time to get them done. Put tasks that require similar handling together. Set time aside to handle correspondence and bill paying. Go through all your catalogs at one sitting. Then fill out your orders and make the phone calls. Buy special-occasion cards at one time. You'll find it easier to remember a friend if you have a supply of cards on hand. Make two batches of stew or soup at the same time. Many of the ingredients are the same, and it's as easy to chop six onions in the food processor as two. Label and freeze portions in microwave containers.

Many people also find their computers are great time savers. Besides helping with record keeping, many programs allow you to set up budgets, prepare tax forms, and access a great deal of information without leaving your den. *Prodigy*® is one of the most varied computer software packages available. In addition to having access to nearly unlimited information, you can also make airline and train reservations, order goods, and open financial accounts. There is time to be saved if you can find a minute to look for it.

Things to Remember About Finding More Time

- Establish priorities. Know what is important to you at home and at work.

- Learn to say no. You can't do everything.
- 80% of the value is in 20% of the items.
- To-do lists really work.
- Learn to delegate appropriate tasks.

5

Early
Family Years

Family

Family. How can one word conjure up so many conflicting emotions? One day the thought of our families can make us feel loved, welcome, and safe. On another day, we might be ready to volunteer for a long-term solo space mission. Perhaps these changing emotions are a key to understanding family. Just as each individual grows and changes, so do family units. The game plan is never constant. Decisions and realities that work one year may not work the next. To find balance with our families is to accept change.

Most of us are in the real middle of family life now. We are trying to raise our children at the same time that we are trying to be good children to our parents. Just as we are showing our personal independence most clearly—raising our children somewhat differently from the way we were raised—we may be caught up in the lives of our aging parents and their new vulnerabilities.

The clearest thing about today's family is that there are many challenges and difficulties and few easy answers. Our family demands will change as our children grow up and as we grow older. Perhaps that is the most important thing to remember in raising children—*this will change*. Whether you are in the middle of the terrible twos or full-scale adolescent rebellion, it's very helpful to try to remember that this stage is temporary. Of course that doesn't mean problems shouldn't concern you and get your immediate attention, but it does mean that today's tantrum-throwing toddler is tomorrow's delightful companion.

The other side of the coin is that those moments of feeling that you've got it all worked out are also temporary. Your kids are happy and thriving, your husband loves you, and work is finally fulfilling. Then the kids hit puberty, your husband hits serious middle age, and your company gets sold. Change.

We have no choice about our first family. We are born into a group of individuals who, for better or worse, shape much of the first quarter of our lives. As we begin to choose our future family life —spouse, friends, children, and sometimes co-workers—we usually use our birth family as some sort of guide.

There are also many factors over which we have little control. Our parents' health, our love of a spouse who will *never* be the president of the local conglomerate, each child's particular and special needs —these are all elements that determine some of the needs we will find in our own lives. In this chapter and the next, we're going to concentrate on two of the toughest situations facing today's families: our children and our parents. The situations are similar in that both are influenced by factors we cannot necessarily control.

Becoming a Parent

It seems as though everybody is becoming a parent. We have all read the articles (and perhaps participated in the trend) about women in their mid- to late 30s having their first children. Many of these original "baby boomers" put off having children while they concentrated on their careers. At the same time, many women born in the generation after the baby boom (now in their late teens and early 20s) are also having children. In fact, we may be in the beginning of yet another "boom." Only 8% of adults aged 18–29 expect to remain childless. Ten years ago, 21% of that same age group said they would have no children. Whatever the reasons, it seems safe to say that the family is alive and well and sure to continue despite the difficuities, sacrifices, and problems associated with being parents.

Becoming a parent is the beginning of a new vocabulary. Besides the specifics of pregnancy, you are now entering the worlds of day care, stay-at-home mom, working parent, househusband, guilt, quality time, boredom, and joy. Articles about the mommy- and daddy-tracks, as well as legislative issues such as family-leave, get your attention as never before. That is, if you have a minute to read about them. Issues and problems that were once theoretical (who will stay home if the baby is sick?) are now right in the middle of your daily, practical real life.

Working Parents

Perhaps the biggest decision facing a couple or woman expecting or wanting a child is, who is going to care for the child in the early years? (Children need care for years, but it's probably not practical to plan more than two or three years at a time. There are many factors that can change.) There is always controversy surrounding "stay-at-home" mothers versus "working" mothers. In reality, it's rarely women who are making these silly divisions. All mothers are working mothers. And fathers do fit into the child-care picture— now more than ever.

The first decision to make is whether one parent can give up his or her job in order to care for the baby. Can you afford to live on the reduced income? Different couples earning the same amount of money answer this question differently. The key is not what other people are doing, but what you and your spouse feel is best for your growing family. Your decision depends on many things. Besides the financial reality, your decision might be influenced by the kind of child care available in your area. Another factor is each person's job and career path. Pay attention to your emotions and accept that they may change. After a few months caring for a child, some people may be eager to get back in the work world. For others, the joy of being with their child is more satisfying than their work. Don't worry if you don't fit someone else's view of what you should be doing. The more planning and talking you and your spouse can do before pregnancy, the better. Some people start savings accounts to help with the financial picture. Others might decide to change jobs, depending upon how their current work fits in with their goals for the family.

Pregnancy and Work

Eighty-five percent of all working women will become pregnant during their working life. In an ideal world, childbirth and child rearing would be an accepted and planned part of the working world. Unfortunately, a pregnant working woman is sometimes treated as though she is an exception, even though she is obviously part of a large majority. It's important to try to think through how your pregnancy might affect your job. For many women, there are no problems at all; for others, because of antiquated or nonexistent maternity and paternity policies, there may be significant difficulties in maintaining your job during and after your pregnancy.

Be sure to research your company's policies as well as those of your husband's employer. If your supervisor does not understand or have copies of the policies or benefits books, talk to someone in human resources or the personnel department.

The Pregnancy and Motherhood Diary by Susan Schiffer Stautberg suggests that working women and their spouses give a lot of thought to how they will try to handle their pregnancy, childbirth, and job *before* informing their bosses and co-workers about the event. Some of the areas she suggests should be given careful thought are:

1. When will you need time off and how much time will you need? In calculating this, include not only your maternity leave but time for doctor's visits and perhaps a shortened workday, or workweek, somewhere along the line.
2. How do you want to account for your time off? Will you take maternity leave only or draw on vacation time as well?
3. When do you plan to return to work?
4. Will you come back full time or would you like to try working at home, job sharing, or part-time employment?

5. How much will you be paid during your absence?
6. How will you keep in touch with the office?

Many of us feel that we have few choices available regarding going back to work, time off, part time versus full time, etc. Unfortunately, some of us do have fewer choices than others. However, by thinking carefully and being a little brave as well as creative, many women find they have more choices than they first expected. Can a part of your job be done from home? If you can show your employer that specific responsibilities can be done from home (you may need special equipment such as a computer and perhaps a fax machine and telephone hookup for your computer), you may be able to establish a full-time job with part-time office hours. The key is to think the possibilities through and approach your employer with the attitude that you've got a solution, not a problem. Pregnancy is a normal, vital part of life.

Know Your Legal Rights

For the many women whose jobs and/or employers offer no room for creativity and negotiation, pregnancy and maternity leave are serious threats to their jobs. In 1978, the Pregnancy and Discrimination Act was passed. It's an amendment to Title VII of the Civil Rights Act of 1964. There are two key elements to this legislation that every working woman should know. One is that employers cannot refuse to hire a pregnant woman, nor can they fire her, or force her to take a leave of absence. In addition, the bill categorizes pregnancy as a disability and states that a pregnant woman is entitled to all benefits that she would get under the company's disability plan, including continuation of health insurance, and the same income and job protection offered to anyone suffering a disability. Unfortunately, many companies don't offer disability plans. In addition, pregnancy is considered a six to eight-week disability, which is not as much time as most women want.

Smaller companies can be the best or, sometimes, the worst place for an expectant family to work. In the ideal situation, a small company can make decisions based on the individual employee's abilities and needs. Flextime can be individualized and there can be more of a team feeling in the entire company, allowing for shifts in work hours and loads to help accommodate the personal needs of all employees. On the other hand, companies with fewer than 15 employees are not subject to federal discrimination laws. Depending upon individual state laws, women can be fired because they are pregnant. In addition, a small staff can make it more difficult for a company to allow for individual flexibility. The key is communicating with your employer and honestly assessing how your pregnancy and delivery will affect your ability to do your job.

Know Your Company

If possible, it's important to know as much as possible about your company's pregnancy and maternity policies before joining the company. Helen Norton, a women's rights attorney, suggests that you ask as many questions as needed in order to understand fully a potential employer's policies and attitudes toward pregnancy. Many women realistically worry that such questions might work against them in the employment process. At the same time, finding the right employer will save much stress, money, and time in the future. If you know that you will want a child in the next few years, think about looking for an employer that will make this decision as easy as possible. As employees exert more pressure on companies to respond to the needs of the family, change will occur. There is competition for the best workers, and the more questions we ask as we look for the right job, the more employers will have to listen.

Child Care

There is a lot of talk about what is best for our children. Many people who suggest that it's best for a child to have the full attention of the mother in the early years often seem to ignore the fact that *choice* in this matter is not valid for many families.

In many instances, financial necessities make it essential for both parents to work. In 1970, 29% of children under five had working mothers. By 1990, that number had increased to 53%. For children 6–17, 43% of their mothers worked in 1970, while 1990 figures show that number to have risen to 66%. In addition, 25% of American households with children under 18 are single-parent households, and the vast majority of these are headed by women. Rather than debate the pros and cons of choice when choice exists for so few of us, it may be more realistic to look at the various alternatives for child care.

The latest statistics available on child care show that in 1987 preschool-age children of working mothers were cared for in the following environments:

Relative	37%
Commercial day care	24%
Neighborhood day care	22%
Other	17%

Finding the right care for your infant and toddler is one of the most difficult choices for today's families. Most of us do not have a family member nearby who is willing or able to care for a child all day, every day. There are approximately 77,000 licensed child-care centers serving 4 million children each day. As we look to day-care companies, both large and small, we see a huge disparity in the quality of care as well as the cost per child.

So What Do We Do?—
Choosing the Right Day Care

There are several kinds of child care available in most areas. Of course, each one of us wants the best for our child, but there are several factors that should be considered before making a final decision. It is important to do your homework well in advance of your back-to-work date. Parents who are happy with their child-care arrangements agree that they did lots of research and interviewing before making the final decision. Another point made by several parents is that their research sometimes made them change their minds about what might be best for their child.

The first question to ask yourself is, what kind of child care do you think you want for your child? Do you want someone to come into your home or do you want to take your child to the caretaker? Caretakers outside the home are usually either businesses set up for child care, programs through a local community organization such as the YMCA, or family caregivers, who are usually one or two people providing day care in their home. Your choices depend upon how many children you have, how many hours you and your spouse work, and whether you can afford your choice. Many mothers (and more fathers) are working part time. While that means fewer hours of day care, it may also narrow your choices since not all outside-the-home care is flexible enough for part-time attendance. Many centers or family care providers must limit their space to those paying a full rate.

It is best to begin researching day-care options in your area as soon as you can. Here are some ideas of places and people to call in your area to get the best information:

1. Anyone you know who has children. Talk with as many parents as possible about their decisions, how they think their children are doing, what they would change if they could, pitfalls and triumphs.

2. Look for information at your local maternity and new-baby shops. In smaller communities particularly, there might be advertisements for child care. Collect as much information as possible.

3. Start a file and organize your search. Separate your information into in-home and away-from-home care. Pay attention to age requirements and limitations. (Even if it doesn't apply to your child now, save it for the future.) This is the time to use all the brains and imagination you've got. Good child-care solutions often involve creativity.

4. Visit as many different child-care centers or homes as possible. This process needn't be too time-consuming. If you don't like what you see, leave. If it looks like a possibility, put it on your follow-through list. You might try to drop by centers early

in the morning, during lunch, or at the end of your day. Besides seeing whether the route is feasible, you'll have a chance to see the center in action during busy hours.

5. You and your spouse can also divide this preliminary stage. If either of you is uncomfortable while visiting a potential care center, take it off your list. Once you've got a list of places to revisit, you should try to coordinate your schedules and go together. The more committed both parents are to specific child-care arrangements, the more smoothly they will be implemented.

At-Home Specifics

All the above suggestions can be used in evaluating someone who might come into your home. Develop your list by talking with others and investigating advertisements. Set up preliminary appointments (best done at your house) and involve your spouse as much as possible. Observe the interviewee interacting with your child. In at-home care, you need to think about transportation in reverse. How convenient is your home to public transportation? If your area is not well served, that will require your caretaker to have her own car or you will have to provide taxi service or public transportation, either paying for it or driving your helper to and from home. If the chosen in-home caretaker has a car and drives to work, do you want her to take your child in the car? If so, is there a proper car seat in the car?

It is very important to have a clear understanding of the responsibilities of your in-home caretaker. Many parents have found it best to have a written job description of what is expected. Not only does that prevent misunderstandings, it gives both of you a place to begin discussions. The biggest area of responsibility is obviously caring for your child. Write down exactly what you mean by that—meals, baths, play time, park time. Even if you do not share your notes with your child's caretaker, it will help you focus on what is important.

After child care, the biggest area of discussion will probably be housekeeping. Depending upon how many children you have and their ages, a good caretaker can also become a valued house-keeper. It's important to talk with your prospective employees about what other duties they would be willing to do. These other duties, if any, will vary depending upon your needs and the skills of your caretaker.

With a new person in the house, it is best to start slowly. Child care is by far your primary desire. Make sure both you and the caretaker remember that. As those responsibilities smoothly develop, you may be able to talk about additional duties. Think about your own career development as you work with someone else. Remember that you are the manager of your home and that with that domain comes the responsibility to treat others with consideration and thoughtfulness. Think about what has made you think well of an employer and copy him or her. Be specific about additional responsibilities and discuss whether there will be a change in salary. Know your hours and be prepared to pay overtime when it is due. Praise a job well done. Point out problems promptly but do not harbor a grudge.

Katherine Phillips, married and the mother of two girls, is also the television and media critic for the *Richmond* (Virginia) *News Leader.* She is expecting her third child. She has used lots of forms of child care and finds that different solutions are best for different times. Her first child had care in the home, her second went to day care, and now that she's expecting her third, she's once again looking into someone to come to her home.

Katherine stresses that for her the most important factor in evaluating a person and/or a place for her children is her own instinct. "Perhaps it is because I am a reporter, but I interview and ask questions until I am absolutely sure that I have a clear picture of what's going on. I always ask for references and check them. And I *always* drop by at an unscheduled time." She also points out that the same location may not be equally good for all the ages that it serves. The facility with wonderful infant care may not be as good for toddlers, and vice versa.

The Pregnancy and Motherhood Diary lists questions for parents to consider for both at-home and out-of-the-home care.

At Home

1. Why are they working as housekeepers, nurses, nannies, or baby-sitters? Is it a career or an interim decision? What is their educational background?

2. What is their basic child-care philosophy? Be specific. Ask "what if" questions.

3. How would they handle their own possible disapproval of the parents' actions? For example, if the working mother is delayed at the office, and the child is old enough to understand, would the caregiver be supportive of the mother's dilemma and reassure the child about her imminent return?

4. What does the caregiver consider his/her strengths and weaknesses?

5. Is the caregiver healthy? Any back trouble? Can she or he physically manage the demands of your child/children?

6. How flexible is she in regard to time off and what vacation time would she expect? Does she want pay if *you* take a vacation?

For Family Care or Care Centers

1. Can you get to the center easily from either your office or your home?

2. What are their hours? What happens if you are late?

3. Is the establishment licensed (know your state requirements)? What are the certifications or educational background of the employees?

4. What are the procedures for medical emergencies? Does anyone have first-aid training? In an emergency, to what hospital would your child be taken?

5. Does the center have a vacation policy? Are they closed on holidays? Do the summer hours differ from the rest of the year?

6. What is the maximum number of children accepted? What is the ratio of adults to children?

7. What is the average stay for employees? If possible, find out what they earn.

These questions just begin to cover the many questions you will have as you choose a caretaker for your child. Remember Katherine Phillips's advice regarding paying attention to your instincts. If something doesn't seem right, then there may well be a problem. If your child can talk, be sure to pay attention to what he or she has to say about the day.

In the beginning, you may feel more comfortable making several day visits to either the center or your home. As you see that things are going smoothly, you and your child will become more comfortable with the schedule. You will need to take time to re-evaluate your choices as your child (and perhaps the size of your family) grows, but as you become more familiar with your needs you will find this complicated process gets easier.

What About Fathers?

For many years, it seemed that all discussions regarding children and working parents were really about working mothers. We read articles about mother's guilt and paid little attention to father's. Happily, fathers are now getting some time and attention regarding the importance of their role in their children's lives. As stated by James A. Levine of the Families and Work Institute in New York, "We're at the very beginning of realizing that work-family conflict is not just a women's issue." Levine conducts seminars called "Daddy Stress" for working fathers. He has found that the biggest stress factors for these family men are:

1. Feeling there's never enough time to be with their kids.
2. Rushing to and from work to drop children off at day care or to pick them up.
3. Facing watchful eyes of bosses and colleagues when leaving work early to go to a kid's baseball game or ballet recital.
4. Taking time off to stay home with a sick child.
5. Having work-related travel cut into family time.

"We're just starting to hear from corporate recruiters about guys raising questions about the travel the job requires," Levine says.

More fathers are feeling the pressures of child care as more women work outside the home. Decisions regarding child care should involve both parents. Not only do fathers have a chance to bond with their children in ways their own fathers might have missed, but the reduced pressure on the mothers will help make the entire family a more cohesive unit. Child-care decisions are difficult in the best of circumstances. Parents need to work together in order to give their children the best that can be found for their particular situation.

Teenagers Can Be Tough

During our focus groups, we heard a common remark among mothers of teenagers: It's hard work. Along with caring for infants and toddlers, being parents of teenagers seems to be one of the biggest sources of stress in today's world. As they enter the teen years, "open" children become withdrawn and "easy" children become difficult. Music and clothing choices are rarely in line with parents' tastes, and often there is at least one close friend who the parents can't stand. The biggest problem, though, is the worry that teenagers think they are grown up and parents know that in some ways they are still children.

The problem seems to have two components. One is the realization that teenagers are physically more independent than younger children and therefore less subject to parental control. Besides worrying about their teenage children driving (and riding with friends), parents of adolescents also worry about their children's exposure to and potential involvement with drugs and sex. As we all know, these can become life-and-death issues. The second part of the problem is that these increased risks occur at a time when children are not interested in talking with, much less confiding in, their parents. This silence only increases a parent's worry.

One creative parent finds that the best time to talk with her teenagers is while she's driving them. They can't leave the room while it's moving at 55 miles an hour. It isn't a guarantee that they will actually engage in conversation, but there is a good chance that your point will be heard. If communication is spotty, try not to lecture. Keep the conversation specific. Try getting them to participate by using questions such as "Are these expectations unrealistic?" and "What time can I expect you home?"

It is essential to negotiate issues of independence and responsibility with our children as they approach adulthood. Try stressing the relationship between independence and responsibility as you look for ways to communicate with your children. There is no reason why privileges such as using the car can't be tied to a responsibility such as doing the grocery shopping (you should provide a detailed list).

The use of alcohol and drugs is neither "cool" nor necessary; while it may be viewed as a rite of passage by some young people, adults do not have to buy into this thinking or look the other way. The statistics on alcohol-related accidents and deaths for school-age children is appalling; the "it won't happen here" attitude is merely ostrich-like.

Parent groups concerned about their teenagers' behavior, but wanting to support their activities constructively, do have choices. Here are two excellent guidelines that we found during our interviews on the topic of parenting.

Guidelines for Hosting Parties

1. Parents should be at home when a party is given and should look in often enough to be in control of the situation. The host family may wish to invite other parents to help chaperone.

2. The host family should establish rules ahead of time and be ready to enforce them.

3. IT IS AGAINST THE LAW TO SERVE ALCOHOLIC BEVERAGES OR MAKE THEM AVAILABLE TO ANYONE UNDER THE AGE OF 21.

4. Drugs should not be available to guests of any age. Guests should not be allowed to bring drugs or alcohol into your home, and those who do so should be told to leave.

5. Parties should be by invitation only and uninvited guests should not be admitted.

6. Specific times should be set for the beginning and end of the party.

7. Hosts should notify the parents of any guest who arrives at the party drunk or under the influence of drugs. Do not let anyone drive under the influence of alcohol or drugs.

Guidelines for Those Attending Parties

1. Means of transportation to and from social events should be agreed upon in advance by parents and children concerned. The type of agreement, of course, depends upon the age of the child. *Emphasize the importance of not driving while under the influence of alcohol or drugs and of not riding with a driver who is under the influence of alcohol or other drugs.*

2. Parents should be encouraged to call a host parent for information about a party such as time, supervision, etc.

3. Parents and their children should exchange phone numbers and know where to reach each other at all times. They should also know when to expect each other home.

4. If your teen is invited to stay overnight with a friend, parents should feel free to talk with the host family beforehand to verify the invitation and find out whether a parent will be home.

Things to Remember
About Family Decisions

- In raising children, remember, *this will change.*
- The key is not what other people are doing, but what you and your spouse feel is best for your growing family.
- Try to know as much as possible about a company's pregnancy and maternity policies *before* joining the company.
- Think about how you will handle pregnancy, childbirth, and the job *before* informing your boss and co-workers about the event.
- Know your legal rights.
- Finding good care for your infant and toddler is one of the most difficult choices for today's families. Give it the time it deserves.

6

Caring for Aging Parents

As people are living longer and healthier lives, it is important to anticipate and realize that many of us are likely to take care of our parents as they grow older. In addition to the benefits of an improved diet and more exercise, our parents are the first generation to reap many of the rewards of 20th-century medical technology. Of course, this also means they are the first generation to suffer both the physical and moral dilemmas of this same technology. There are joint replacements, bypasses, transplants, and lasers to mend many formerly crippling or fatal disorders. All this means that, as children, we too are faced with new challenges, and these challenges come just as we are recognizing that we already have too much to handle.

As our parents get older, our relationship with them changes. The shift of who's dependent on whom can occur gradually and naturally or suddenly—brought on by the death of one parent or a serious illness or fall. There is little we can do to anticipate the exact moment—often there isn't one—when our parents' needs become more of a responsibility in our lives. The time will come when our parents begin to need us for more than love and visits with the grandchildren. The time will come when they need us to help with the daily carrying on of their lives. In short, we may find we are taking care of them more than they are taking care of us. There are a few things we can do to be prepared for this major transition in our lives. Of course, there are no absolutes, but here are a few general ideas to help you add this responsibility to your already full lives.

The most important thing we can do to be ready for this change in our relationship with our parents is to accept that it may well happen. Putting our heads in the sand and not thinking about our parents' aging and eventual death is only going to make the actuality more difficult. We may also be robbing ourselves of potentially rewarding changes in our relationship with our parents. Just as we needed them to face the reality of our becoming 16 and wanting more freedom, they need us to face the reality of their becoming senior citizens.

Noticing the changes in our parents' lives can be a matter of listening a little closer, watching a little more attentively. Are your parents less social than before? Are they going out less with friends, missing church more often, not hearing the phone ring? All these deviations from usual behavior might be important signs of physical or life-style changes. Not going out as much could mean that driving has become a worry, particularly driving at night. It might also be a sign that many of their friends are ill or deceased. Not going to worship services, if that was once an important activity, might be a sign of depression (or, again, driving problems). And not answering the telephone could be the result of hearing loss.

By noticing the problems, you can help your parents adjust to their changing life-style. Ask them, casually, if they are comfortable driving at night. Find out about cabs or driving services in their area and, if possible, offer to pick them up for family events. If you can, speak with someone at their church to see if a ride to and from services can be arranged. For hearing problems, you can help arrange an appointment with a specialist, but also helpful are telephones equipped with special lights, bells, and amplifiers for the hearing-impaired.

In-Town or Long-Distance Child
—Neither Is Easy

Every family is different, but for many of us there is the dilemma of trying to keep up with and take care of our parents from a distance. Many of us live and work in cities far from our parents' home. The long-distance child must make certain adjustments particular to her situation as well as her parents' needs. For example, the regular Sunday-afternoon phone call may no longer be enough contact to know accurately how your parents are doing. Try calling at different times. Calling in the morning and late afternoons during the week may give you a better sense of how your parents' lives are going. Frequently, our parents do not want to tell us about their difficulties. It's easier for them to sound cheerful and in control during a routine and expected call than in an unexpected one. By calling more often, we can keep up with their daily (or weekly) lives and find it easier to notice unwelcome changes.

A daughter in California was unaware that her mother in Georgia was no longer playing bridge on Wednesday afternoons until a chance phone call made her mother confess that the group had broken up because they were all either too crippled or too forgetful to get together. Another long-distance child discovered his parents were having problems with home maintenance when he called to discover his mother upset with his 80-year-old father, who was trying to clean out the gutters. In neither case could the adult child directly help the parent; besides distance, the daughter hated bridge and the son paid someone to clean his own gutters. But, with some creative problem-solving, both were able to help their parents out.

The daughter called a couple of the card-ladies' children and together they came up with a plan that provided a twice-monthly visit for the old friends. In return for the in-town help from the children of her mother's friends, the out-of-town child paid for more than her share of the luncheon costs. The man in this case had never lived in the city where his parents were now living. He did, however, have the yellow pages for the city and was therefore able to find a home-maintenance service located near his parents and arrange for regular service at a fixed cost.

One of the most important things you can do as a long-distance child is to be familiar with the resources where your parents live. Besides having the telephone books, it's a good idea to have the telephone numbers of your parents' friends, doctors, neighbors, and emergency services. You might also think about getting mailings from your parents' church, local community group, and any senior-citizen agencies in their area to help you keep up with services that might be of interest or help to your parents. It's also a good way to let your parents know that you are interested in their activities.

Living in the Same Town as Your Parents

Living near your parents may lessen some of the frustrations caused by being far away, but it can also increase their demands on you. The daughter or son living nearby is frequently burdened with many requests such as accompanying parents on doctors' appointments or doing the weekly (or daily) grocery shopping. The issue is not whether one is willing to do these tasks but how a son or daughter can fit these duties in with the demands already in place. Taking care of parents is particularly hard on the already-burdened single mother. Besides having little or no support raising her children, she is often thought of as the natural caretaker to her parents. There is a subtle but unfair assumption that single adults—whether they have children or not—have more time to take care of their parents than their married sisters or brothers.

It is very important for siblings to be honest and open with each other during times of difficulty with aging parents. Long-distance and in-town siblings need to be aware of the particular difficulties for each child. The out-of-town child is usually suffering from guilt —guilt caused by not being there and sometimes by being relieved that she is not there. The toughest thing for the in-town relative is that the vast burden of caretaking falls upon her. It's very important for relatives to discuss some of the common patterns of behavior that can occur.

One of the most common and potentially most hurtful situations is the return of the prodigal son or daughter. Parents make a big to-do about a distant sibling's semiannual visit while the children providing daily care and friendship are taken for granted. It's important for siblings to get out their frustrations with each other. It is much easier to help parents and perhaps convince them of the need for a change when the children speak in a united voice.

As an out-of-town child, if your parents start telling you that your sister doesn't understand, try to hold off from voicing an opinion until you have had a chance to talk with her. Chronic problems can be disguised for a day or two, and your sister may well be more familiar with the situation. Don't be the whirlwind sibling who pops into town and tries to solve long-standing problems overnight— even if you can. Take care to realize that you may see solutions because you are not there every day. Share your thoughts with your siblings. Say things like "What do you think about . . . ?" instead of "The thing to do is . . ."

Another problem is that in-town siblings may keep information from out-of-town children. This can be just as unfair as someone barging in and changing an established routine. If you don't share the problems and your worries with your siblings, it's impossible to expect them to understand what you go through. It's also important to share medical and financial information. If a parent seems to have a special relationship with one of your brothers or sisters, try to be open with that sibling about how best to operate. For example, if your mother only wants to discuss money matters with your older brother—even though you work in finance and your brother works for the government—talk the situation over with your brother and let him find out the needed information for the two of you to share.

What If They Have to Move?

Our parents live in many situations. Some are still in the house we were brought up in. Others have moved to a new city as a result of work and/or retirement. Still others may be living in reduced circumstances, counting on social security for all or most of their financial support. Whatever the circumstance, many of us will be faced with the difficult problem of realizing that our parents can no longer live on their own. It isn't always easy to determine that one or both parents must be moved. Here are a few key questions suggested by Eugenia Anderson-Ellis and Marsha Dryan in *Aging Parents and You:*

1. Has your parent's health changed dramatically in recent weeks, months?

2. Can they take care of personal and hygiene needs such as dressing and shaving?

3. Can (and do) they prepare meals and feed themselves?

4. Can they handle bill paying, bank matters? Have they been the victim of a scam involving money?

5. Can they handle the day-to-day physical requirements of their home such as climbing the stairs, reaching food in the cabinets or pantry, operating the stove and other appliances?

6. Can (and do) they take medication properly in terms of both amount and frequency?

7. Are they oriented as to who and where they are? Could they call for help and give their address?

8. Are they continent?

9. Is their neighborhood still safe?

Sometimes a sudden accident or illness will precipitate the need to move our parents somewhere else. At other times the change is more gradual. If we are lucky, our parents will anticipate growing older and initiate some changes while they can. That is, they will think about finding a place to live with fewer steps and more public transportation. If you can, talk to your parents about their particular situation and let them know that you are ready for changes they may decide to make. Some children inadvertently slow down their parents' decision-making by being unwilling to accept the changes themselves. "Oh, but, Mom, I can't stand to think of another family moving into our house—you can't sell it" or "But, Daddy, if you move to Florida with your friends, when will the grandchildren ever see you? You don't really want a retirement community, do you?" Try not to confuse your own desires with the needs of your parents.

Here is a checklist from *Aging Parents and You*. It is not just things to do but also includes things to think about. It's an excellent help in beginning to talk with your parents and other family members about change.

1. Decide on who will be the primary caregiver.

2. Agree on how caretaking roles will be divided.

3. Be clear on who will pay for care (and who will take charge of the often-confusing insurance forms).

4. Find out where all essential papers are kept: deeds, insurance, wills, funeral plans. It is much easier to become familiar with these business details before an emergency.

5. Review the options: living at home with multiple support systems, living with someone else, living in a community catering to the elderly, or living in an institution.

6. Know the resources available in your parents' community. Is there adult day care, meal programs, or emergency medical care?

7. Determine whether moving in with an adult child is an option for your parents.

8. Consider the availability of alternative housing: foster care, board-and-care homes, or group homes.

As you wrestle with the changing living situation of one or more elderly parents it's very important to share your problems and feelings with others. Even if you are lucky and have siblings with whom you are close, it's important to find some individual support outside your own family network. Perhaps one of the more important social changes that has occurred over the past decades is the growth of the support group. There are groups for nearly every imaginable problem. Call your local churches, hospitals, nursing homes, and retirement centers and ask about groups in your areas. If you can't find one, think of starting one. These groups will allow you to know that you are not alone. By listening to and sharing with others some of the day-to-day problems as well as some of your own feelings, you will be helping yourself cope. Remember too, others have been there before—learn from them.

One final point. This is an excellent time to make sure your own plans for the future are realistic. Do you have a will? Have you thought about retirement? Do you know where you want to live? Discuss all these things with your spouse and children (once they are in their teens).

Time Together,
the Making of a Family

Most of this chapter has discussed the problems of being part of a family. Try not to focus on only the problems of family life. It's important to remember that a strong family can be one of our greatest resources and refuges in life. What makes a strong family? If we come from one, how do we perpetuate it? If our first family was damaging, how do we learn to build a new model for ourselves and our loved ones?

An important factor in building a strong family is to understand that it is an ongoing process. You cannot wait until the children are older to begin talking with them about their day and their friends. You and your spouse need to talk about what you want for your family and how you can achieve these goals. Building a family is not something to do tomorrow—it is a continuing series of choices and decisions. "Family first" is a meaningless motto unless the commitment to the family is firm and visible.

There are some simple things a family can do to establish and strengthen the bonds between members.

1. Starting when your children are born, make sure they know they are part of a family. Talk about it, show them pictures, and try to keep them in touch with at least some of your extended family. Reinforce relationships.

2. Eat dinner together as often as possible. Besides offering a chance for everyone to hear each other's news, shared meals create a deeper closeness among people. If the children drive you crazy (different reasons at different ages), don't quit. If your children are young, you can cut back to a couple of nights a

week, but don't give up. This is particularly important during the teen years. It may be the one time every day you can touch base with your kids.

3. Include the children in important discussions or decisions. If there are financial difficulties, let the kids know. If it means changes in their life-style (new school, new house), they should be prepared.

4. Don't avoid problems. If you or a member of your family has a problem—school or work, drugs or alcohol—get some help. There are many pressures on kids and adults, and most families seek out professional help at least once.

5. Have some fun together! Find something that everyone likes —it doesn't matter what: putt-putt golf, going to the lake or beach, watching street performers at a local crafts fair, whatever works for your family. Establish rituals of fun and reinforce these rituals year after year. These are the things that have a good chance of bringing everyone back in balance and keeping family members in touch with one another.

6. Child abuse is a problem for some parents. Crisis or support services for parents, such as helplines, hotlines, drop-in centers and self-help groups like Parents Anonymous, now exist for help. Prevention education for children has also been instituted. Children may be taught how to say "no" in the face of abuse and to report threats. Programs also focus on developing self-esteem, conflict-resolution skills, and adult-child and peer-peer relations as tools in self-protection.

7. Let your family know you love them.

Things to Remember About
Caring for Aging Parents
and Making a Family

- It is important to be prepared for and accept the changes in your relationship with your parents. Putting your head in the sand and not thinking about your parents' aging and eventual death is only going to make the actuality more difficult.

- By noticing the problems as they occur, you can help your parents adjust to their changing life-style.
- Long-distance and in-town siblings need to be aware of the particular difficulties for each child.
- One of the most important things you can do as a long-distance child is to be familiar with the resources where your parents live.
- Talk to your parents about their particular situation and let them know that you are ready for any changes they may decide to make.
- Establish family rituals of fun and reinforce these rituals year after year.

7

Working for Others

Work

"Work" is one of the most common words in our language; it is also one of the most complex. Work means many things. It can be a place, a task, a job, or a career. It can be frustrating or fulfilling. It can make us financially secure and provide us with a greater sense of self-worth, or lead us into bankruptcy and depression. For some, work is a calling. We frequently hear stories of writers and artists knowing as small children what they wanted to do with their lives. Others follow the examples of their mothers and fathers. Many police and fire departments are staffed by sons and, increasingly, daughters of veterans of these forces. We've all seen family businesses (and occasionally read of bitter in-fighting among family members). Most of us are less directed as we begin our working lives. For most of us, work is a series of jobs that may or may not have anything to do with what we studied in high school or college. One job leads to another. However we get there, it's important to recognize that work is part of most of our lives and it deserves our thoughts and attention.

Two-thirds of all Americans age 16 or over are currently working or looking for work. Nearly two-thirds of all married couples are two-paycheck families. By 1988, 56.6% of all women were working outside the home and 45% of all working people were women. No wonder more and more Americans are beginning to feel that they work in order to live instead of the reverse. Work has become financially essential for most of us. Home ownership and having and educating children were once goals that were often achievable on one income, the man's. That has changed. Today, it takes two incomes to achieve the same goals. Most of us work because we need the money. The luxury of finding a job that fulfills us is being edged out and replaced by the necessity to find work—any work.

The average full-time worker spends 44 hours a week at work. Add to this the amount of work taken home, and the full-time number rises to 46 hours. The part-time worker works about 23 hours per week. The longest hours are reported by executives making over $50,000 a year. Another group working more hours than the average are those who are self-employed. The benefits of working for yourself are many, as we'll discuss in the next chapter; but working fewer hours is rarely one of them.

There are some who distinguish between a job and a career. Whatever you call it, it is work. Rather than debate distinctions, we think it's best for everyone to think in terms of skills and experience. Whether you recognize it as such, you probably have a specialty. There are skills in which you excel that most likely have a professional application. Work experience is often as valuable as school work. If you are a career changer, moving from teaching into business, many of the skills that you honed while teaching will be valuable in business. Anyone who can handle a room of 25 children can certainly do well in a fast-paced business. Of course, if you want to be a lawyer, you must have a law degree. But there are many careers built from everyday job experiences and the smarts to know how to pull them together. Careers are made by people just like you.

Work can make you feel great; it can also make you feel terrible—and the same job can do both. Work is inevitable for all but the tiniest number of us. Where does it fit in a balanced life and are there ways to help it fit better? These are not easy questions. For many, balance is improved by having more money; for others, the key to balance is more time. It would be great if the choices were only ours to make, but of course they're not. At the same time, we have a better chance of being happy if we know that we've done our best to find the job that best fits our needs. No job is perfect. We quit striving for perfection in the first chapter. But if we have a good idea of what is important to us—career, being with our children, money, health benefits, etc.—we can make decisions about our work that will give us more control and balance.

In the next two chapters we will discuss some of the issues and trends taking place in the work force. As you read, be aware of how you feel about your work. Are you happy at your job? What makes you happy? Do you like what you are doing more than you did five years ago? Do you want to be doing the same thing in five years? Are you happy with the amount of money you make? Perhaps more important than your particular answers is the fact that you are asking the questions.

If answering these basic questions about your job makes you realize that you want something else, you can begin to plan the next phase of your career. On the other hand, if your answers make you satisfied that what you are doing is what you want to be doing, you can congratulate yourself on your luck and skill in handling your career and know that this part of your life is currently in order.

Work usually occupies different places in our lives at different times in our lives. We may feel that the company we join at 20 is where we will be working all our lives, but that's rare in today's world. Most of us change and grow; we marry and have children; companies either expand or decline; our expenses increase and opportunities arise. At 20, we may be more concerned with the social aspects of work than the pension plan, while at 50 there are few of us who *won't* ask detailed questions about retirement plans.

Most of us will decide or be forced to rethink our job strategy at least once during our working lives. For many of us, these changes will occur somewhat frequently. Whether you are thinking of change now or just wondering if you are doing the most with what you've got, there are some skills that are necessary in nearly every job. Whatever you are doing now, whether you are content with your job or looking for something different, these are skills that you should evaluate for yourself.

The following list of job skills comes from Louise McNamee, a top advertising agency executive. They are applicable to all workers concerned about finding success and satisfaction at work:

1. *Communicating*. It's impossible to think of a job that doesn't require the ability to communicate. Read your letters and see if they are clear and to the point. Listen to yourself on the telephone. Notice the things that make you enjoy talking with someone else. Also make note of telephone habits that annoy you. Make sure you are not guilty of similar behavior.

2. *Listening*. Don't get so involved in telling someone what you are doing that you forget to listen.

3. *Planning*. "Look before you leap!" You will get more done if you have a plan of action. This applies to any business at any level. A plan can be devised in as short a time as 30 seconds—"I'll return my phone calls before starting on the report"—or might take a full day or longer, depending upon the complexity of the project. Get in the habit of consciously deciding what you are going to do and in what order.

4. *Building relationships*. Everyone prefers to work with people who are easy to get along with. That doesn't mean you have to be a joke-teller or a yes person, but do be aware of the need for consideration of others while on the job.

5. *Being comfortable with change*. For some of us, change is exciting; it keeps us alert. We love learning new things. For others, change can be threatening, especially if we are happy with the way things are. Try to accept that change, both good and bad, is inevitable in the workplace. If your department is implementing new systems and procedures that you *know* are wasting time and money, it's still almost always best to "get with the program" and learn the new ways.

What's Best for You—
Large, Medium, or Small?

The Strengths of Corporate Life

There's a lot of talk around about "domos," the *downwardly mobile*. There are articles about people quitting their jobs, cutting back on their hours, and learning that they can only get so much gratification from an expensive foreign car. These reports tend to share something else in common: One of the working partners in the scaled-back partnership is usually described as "happy as a corporate attorney" or "partner in a downtown financial company." It's a lot easier to scale back when one of you has a job that provides health insurance, a pension plan, savings programs, and, occasionally, health clubs, sabbatical programs, and tuition reimbursement.

Working for a big company can be a tremendous benefit in balancing your life. Most importantly, there are usually excellent job opportunities and a great deal of room for career advancement in large corporations. They can offer strong training programs in many fields, and you will frequently be working with some of the top talent in the country. In addition, there's the fun of working in a company that can afford up-to-date office equipment and has the resources to keep everything running. It is easier to be efficient with the aid of mail rooms, corporate expense accounts, and technical backup. If you've ever tried to copy, collate, and assemble a 40-page report with graphs, you'll appreciate the copy machines that do everything but write the report for you.

Large corporations are also beginning to adjust to the needs of today's family. Slowly, we are seeing more big companies offer parental as well as maternity leave. More employees are given the option to scale back their work load to help with child-care needs without jeopardizing their benefits. Work reforms are coming and, because of the size of their work force, big companies will be among the early advocates.

There are many other advantages to working for a large company. The training they can offer allows employees the chance to broaden and expand their individual skills. Working for a well-known company brings instant respectability to your resume. If you or your partner is considering taking or leaving a job for one of these companies, be sure to weigh all the good points.

The downside to working for a large company depends a lot on the personality of the individual employee. Internal politics and procedural red tape (such as filling out two forms in triplicate in order to get a calendar for a new employee) are more stressful to some of us than to others. Some people feel that large companies are impersonal and that it is difficult to have full control over a project. Once again, balance is best achieved by knowing both what you want and what environment works best for you. For many people, internal politics are easily tolerated because of the excellent benefits.

Medium and Smaller-Size Companies

Perhaps the best thing about smaller companies is the opportunity to know everyone, from the president to the night security guard. For many of us, small companies provide the opportunity to know our company's product or service from start to finish, as opposed to having our involvement limited to one small piece of the whole. If you like being involved, or at least in touch, with every part of a company's operation, look for opportunities in smaller firms.

Another possible advantage in a company with fewer employees is a chance at more flexible financial incentives. Small companies may have more flexibility in tailoring benefit programs and incentive plans. They are also excellent learning grounds if you think you would ever like to own or run your own company. The experience of working for a successful small business is invaluable for your own venture. Take the opportunity to learn how the financial system is set up, when the bills get paid, what the budget looks like. Pay attention to the office equipment and try to become involved in the decisions surrounding purchases of computers, copy machines, and phone systems.

Is Your Job at Risk?

No matter who you are or how long you have been with your company, it is always a good idea to assess and evaluate your job and the likelihood of its disappearing. Unfortunately, a solid performance at work will no longer guarantee a place in the company and a regular paycheck. Many people have lost their jobs while being told that their work was good. Neither is longevity necessarily a shield against termination. The fact that you've been with the company for ten years is not a reason to think your job is safe. It's important to be realistic about your company and your future in it.

Your job can disappear in two ways. One, you can be replaced. That is, you will be let go and someone else will be hired (or promoted) to do the same job. Two, your job can be abolished, wiped out. Jobs are usually eliminated to save money. They can also be lost as a consequence of a merger or takeover resulting in duplicate departments—few companies need two sections with responsibility for the same thing. It's wise to prepare for the worst. In today's world there is very little job security. There are a few things you can do that will help you feel as secure as is possible in today's world and be prepared should your job ever be in jeopardy:

1. *Try to get a written job description or a set of objectives for your position.*   Having responsibilities documented is vital in helping you show management why you are a valuable employee. Keep your communications with your supervisor on the right track.

2. *Do everything you can to get an annual written performance review.*   Most companies have a policy on performance reviews. If yours doesn't, or if your supervisor hasn't given you one, it's perfectly acceptable to ask for it. You can even use the former mayor of New York's "How am I doing?" line. It's critical to get feedback on your performance. The most important feedback is what you need to do to improve.

3. *Review your own files.*   Keep your own files up-to-date and go through your files with an eye to your own future elsewhere, even if that day never comes. Make copies of reports, projects,

and campaigns showing your talents. Not only can these be good samples to show prospective employers, they are also good reminders of your accomplishments as you work on a new resume.

4. *Copy your Rolodex or address list.* If you ever have to conduct a new job search, your Rolodex is one of your strongest resources.

5. *Review your finances and share your concerns with your partner.* As difficult as it may be to face the possibility of losing your job, you'll feel better if you know exactly where you stand. Few of us have the recommended six months of salary in a savings account. Now is the time to try to bolster what savings you do have and think twice about taking on any new debt.

What to Do If You Are Fired or Laid Off

No matter what the circumstances, losing one's job is a traumatic experience. Perhaps the most important thing to remember if it happens to you is that you are not alone. Millions of people are fired or lose their jobs every year. Many go on to better jobs, and it's not unusual to hear that getting fired was "the best thing that ever happened." Of course, those of us who have been fired know that these words are of little help in the first days following the bad news. Be honest about your feelings, but try not to dwell on the past. Learn from the experience and move on.

The only good thing to come from the recent termination of a large number of people is that there are now many books, groups, and companies out there to help. An excellent book is *When Smart People Fail* by Linda Gottlieb and Carol Hyatt. It's full of stories and examples of people who have succeeded after "failing." No story is more dramatic than Linda Gottlieb's. Fired after 20 years with the same television company, she went on to make "Dirty Dancing," one of the most successful independent films ever made. Reading about how others faced the difficulties of being out of work can help you in two ways. You'll see that you are not alone and you may pick up some pointers on a job search by learning how others tackled the problem.

It's fine to show your disappointment at losing your job, but it's important not to burn bridges. Work communities are small, and stories are frequently repeated. Accounts of destroyed files and temper tantrums are not the way you want others to hear that you need a new job. Handling this tough situation with poise and calm will impress others and prove your professionalism. If you need to express your anger, try to do it outside the business community. Talk to your spouse and good friends. Get the anger out, put it behind you, and get on with the new job hunt. Or, as Lee Iacocca has said, take your anger and turn it into positive energy.

There can be a silver lining in losing your job. While most of your day will be spent on the new job search, you can set aside some time to do the things you never had time to do when you were working full time. You can improve your house and pursue a hobby. This is a great time to begin an exercise program. Not only will it help prevent depression and weight gain, it will also give you a sense of control over your life. You don't have to be miserable.

What to Do If Your Partner Loses a Job

As personally difficult as it is to lose a job, it's also very tough on the whole family. Besides the obvious financial effects of unemployment, there are also the problems of depression, tension, and general bad moods that can make family life difficult. In *Out the Organization*, Madeleine and Robert Swain have suggestions on how a spouse can be of help in this tough time:

1. Help you partner avoid negative people. If certain family members or friends always want to talk about the grim job market or why they think your partner lost his job, this is the time to cut back on the time spent with them. If you must see them and they bring up the subject, change topics.

2. Try to keep a moderately active social schedule and do the things you used to do. If a favorite activity is too costly right now, give it up gracefully and try to think of affordable substitutes.

3. Urge your spouse to talk about the job search. Encourage him to make and carry out a daily to-do list. Remember that looking for a job is very hard work. Your spouse's ego is on the line every day, and there will be rejections. Try to find the happy medium between cheerleader and nag.

4. Share the truth with interested friends and colleagues, without dwelling on the negatives. Don't hide the fact that your spouse is looking for a new position; you never know where one might develop. More jobs are found through friends of friends than through newspaper advertisements.

5. Concentrate on being realistic, resourceful, and patient. Show warmth and affection—you are your spouse's best ally.

6. Don't be jealous if your spouse now has time to spend on a hobby. A confident, well-rested individual has a much better chance to get a job than an irritable, tense, desperate candidate.

7. Work with your spouse to decide how to talk to your children. Unless they are very young, they will sense the changes at home. Explain what's going on and reassure them that everything is all right.

Losing a job is a stressful, difficult situation. Be sure to remind yourself of that as you struggle with the daily effects of unemployment. Look for resources in your community to aid you both spiritually and practically. Many churches or community groups have specific gatherings for job seekers. Besides being excellent sources for specific job information, these meetings give you a chance to speak freely with those who will best understand the roller coaster of emotions that accompany the changes brought on by involuntary changes in employment.

Fulfillment Through Work

The more choices we are able to make about what we do for work, the more likely we are to be rewarded and fulfilled by our efforts. While it is impossible to be in control of our careers at all times, we should recognize that *we* are the most important factor in finding personal fulfillment through work. There will be setbacks—many of us will be fired at least once in our lives—but there will also be opportunities. We need to learn to recognize and take advantage of the opportunities as they come our way. Don't be held back by what you *think* you can do. Exceed your own expectations. Learn to know what matters *to you* and worry less about what you think matters to others. Be your own career counselor and ask yourself where you excel and where you are happy. Be realistic about weaknesses and make an effort to improve skills that you know are weak. Share your thoughts with colleagues and family—they may be able to help you see strengths that you overlooked. Balance is a matter of sharing. Share your frustrations as well as your hopes and dreams with those who care about you.

It is important to see work as an ally to a fulfilling life and not an obstacle. The reason many find fulfilling jobs only after being fired is that only then were they forced to ask themselves the questions regarding what they *really* wanted. As we learn to think of work as a lifelong involvement and not just a financial necessity, we are on the road to claiming our lives for ourselves.

Things to Remember About Work

- Work has become financially essential for most of us.
- Many careers are built from everyday job experiences and the ability to pull them together.
- Different-size companies have their own set of advantages and disadvantages. Decide which is best for you.
- Job security is declining in this country. Be prepared to lose your job. If it happens, try to see the challenge in the future —not the mistakes of the past.

8

Going into Business for Yourself

For many of us, the idea of working for ourselves seems to be the best way to achieve balance. Both men and women list owning a business among their top-five dream jobs. We fantasize about making our own hours, being paid what we think we're worth, and not having any problems with a boss. We dream of freedom. Sounds great, but is that a real view of entrepreneurship? What are the trade-offs? The benefits? Is it right for you?

Statistics from the Small Business Administration show that it takes from ten months to two years for a new business to show a profit. In addition, approximately one out of every four businesses fails within two years. It's easy for a new business to become a "black hole" into which you throw all your time, energy, and savings. The very flexibility that was a goal of starting your own business easily can be lost in the tremendous demands of running a new business. It's also important to remember that in a one-person company, you do everything.

The following quiz is designed to help you evaluate your personality and work skills as they apply to having your own business. It was created by Dr. Adele Scheele, a career strategist and management consultant, and was featured in *Working Woman* magazine, January 1991.

Answer each question on a scale from 1 to 10. One means "never" and 10 means "always." Answer the questions honestly. If you've never hired anyone, don't assume you'll be great at it. Like any job skill, it's one that develops over time.

1. Have I managed projects without supervision?
2. Do I initiate projects and carry them through successfully?
3. Have I enjoyed being in charge?
4. Can I hire and fire others when necessary?
5. Can I delegate work?
6. Do I criticize others' work when necessary—and get what I need?
7. Can I negotiate and compromise without feeling that I'm selling out?
8. Do I have abundant energy?
9. Can I delay gratification—put off buying luxuries, and even some basic necessities—to attain a goal?

If you have consistent 9s and 10s, you may be ready to make your dream a reality. For those with some high numbers and some low numbers, take heart. The answers with the lower scores indicate areas that need to be strengthened in order to improve your chances of surviving on your own. You can do this by taking more risks in your current job and looking for classes that might strengthen specific skills such as negotiation and financial planning.

Sharing Your Skills with a Partner

Another way to think about going into business for yourself is to consider doing it with one or two partners. Frequently, companies are formed by colleagues leaving a big company and going out on their own. The advantages of partnerships are many. Skills can be pooled to make both of you stronger together than as individuals. Financial risks can be shared, thus reducing personal liabilities. Perhaps one of the greatest advantages to a partnership is that it allows you the greatest possibilities for balancing the demands of your life.

Gail and Marilyn were both owners of small, successful, public relations firms in Phoenix. Neither one had time to do anything but work. They met at a business luncheon and, after several talks, decided to join forces. They now are co-owners of the fifth-largest firm in Arizona. They have both benefited from the merger because their life-styles require different schedules. Marilyn is married with a child. Gail is single and owns and trains several horses. Marilyn gets to the office around 7:30 A.M. and leaves at approximately 3:30 P.M. Gail arrives about 10 A.M. and is at the office until at least 6 P.M. With this schedule, Marilyn has afternoons at home with her daughter and Gail has mornings to exercise her horses.

For many people, working with a spouse in a family-owned business has been the answer to creative scheduling. They can schedule family demands along with those of their business. The separation between work and home is minimized, and frequently the same relationship that makes the marriage good also works to the good of their company. Obviously, not all married partners would make good business partners. It depends upon the needs and desires of each individual. For some of us, work is work and home is home and never the twain shall meet. For others, working with a spouse on a joint venture strengthens commitment and provides motivation lacking in traditional work situations.

Here are some questions from *Side-by-Side Strategies: How Two-Career Couples Can Thrive in the Nineties* by Jane Hershey Cuozzo and S. Diane Graham. Discuss them with your spouse prior to deciding whether you want to take the plunge together—again. Remember, what you're trying to find out is whether you and your husband can be more balanced by combining your work skills.

1. How well did each of you get along with your family while growing up? Did you find it relatively easy to take part in chores

and projects with family and siblings? Were you more jealous than usual when a brother or sister achieved success?

2. Do you and your spouse have a high efficiency level when it comes to handling your personal business affairs? If one of you is the primary organizer, how easily could you teach the other the ropes? Would the other partner be willing to learn?

3. What skills and talents would each of you bring to the venture? Are your potential contributions complementary, or would there be a fair amount of overlapping?

4. Seeing each other in a professional as well as personal dimension has two sides. Can you accept your spouse's management style even if it differs from your own?

5. Can you sweat out the books together or handle a tough negotiation on Friday night and still want to make love on Saturday morning?

6. Are there currently shared activities in your marriage that have nothing to do with your work lives? It's critical to have outside interests that allow you to spend time together away from the shop.

7. If you have children, or plan to have children, how will working together affect your family life? Do you see your offspring making a contribution? How will you both react if the older children show little or no interest in your company?

8. Are you and your spouse able to evaluate situations and accept failure without blaming the other? Is each of you prepared professionally in case the venture does not succeed, or the other partner wants out? What might such a decision do to your feelings for your spouse?

9. What are your motivations for going into business? What does each of you expect to gain from working together? How similar are your goals for the future?

10. Is each of you committed to the enterprise? Does your loyalty to each other supersede devotion to your company's success?

There are many things to consider before going into business with your marriage partner. No matter how close you are and how well you work together, it is a good idea to make sure that each of you has some responsibilities that don't overlap. Regardless of love, there is ego to take into account. We need to have separate accomplishments in which we take pride.

The Best of Both Worlds: An Entrepreneur Within a Corporation

Besides company ownership, with or without our spouses, or corporate employment, many people have chosen the career path often described as the "best of both worlds." Their choice is to be an independent worker within the context of a larger corporation. There are several ways of achieving this career path, but they share a few common benefits.

1. Your hours are flexible because you are the boss.
2. You have the benefit of corporate support, especially in the areas of advertising and marketing.
3. You are able to share in an information network with others in the same business. Even though you are working on your own, you are not denied the value of colleagues and the opportunity to share knowledge and ideas.

Perhaps the best known and most popular business ideas in this category are franchise operations, real-estate sales, and direct sales. These career tracks are particularly popular among mothers because of the flexibility of hours. Female franchisers control at least 11% of the market. That statistic is particularly remarkable since before 1970 there were virtually no women running franchise businesses.

In addition to being an attractive alternative from a parent's point of view, franchise companies are beginning to seek out mothers as ideal franchise operators. The big companies know that in addition to many women's having lots of business experience, mothers seem ideal because of their stability and motivation. If a woman can successfully work and raise children, it is easy to conclude that she is going to be inspired to make the best of the opportunity.

Real estate, especially residential real estate, has long been a favorite choice for mothers. Once again, a key attraction is flexible times.

A woman can arrange her daily appointments to coincide with her free time. She can continue to be able to pick up the car pool or lead the brownie troop, as well as earn a living. Most real-estate operations also offer their salespeople an office from which to work, and backup and support in the form of secretaries and paralegals. In some cases, these office expenses are paid by the salesperson in a monthly service fee. In others, the support is offset by the commission levels.

As in real estate, direct sales offer a limitless earnings potential. A company like Avon has long been a pioneer in hiring and promoting women, and offers a much larger group of colleagues for an individual sales representative to use as resources than many smaller businesses can offer. Perhaps the biggest advantage of being an Avon sales representative is the chance to develop sales skills within the nurturing environment of a company dedicated to training. You have a chance to see if you like working on your own, without having the expensive start-up costs of franchises or the licensing requirements of real-estate agents.

As with any situation where earnings can vary, a drawback to independent businesses is the uncertainty about monthly or weekly earnings. Some businesses are more sensitive to the economy than others. Real-estate sales is certainly a business of fluctuating incomes, as is any business where earnings are based 100% on commission. A person might have commissions of $15,000 one month and nothing the next, and the next.

Be realistic when looking at the possibility of working for yourself. In addition to the earnings fluctuations, independent workers should be aware of the increased responsibility for tax and social security payments and the lack of pension and retirement plans. There are also the costs of health insurance and disability plans to consider. Talk to experts in these areas in order to understand all sides and costs of the venture. Don't forget to think about costs for accounting and, if necessary, legal services. Remember, you may also need property and liability insurance. Be sure to discuss your plans with people who are in similar fields. If possible, talk to people who tried working for themselves and failed. They are undoubtedly experts in the potential problem areas and might be able to give you valuable tips and warnings.

Part-Time Work

Many couples with children are finding part-time work the best solution for balancing time between raising children and earning money. Part-time work is certainly a good option for mothers during the child-raising years. Charlotte Canape has written a book called *The Part-Time Solution: The New Strategy for Managing Your Career While Managing Motherhood.* The book explores many of the advantages of part-time work, including more time for and less stress in raising children. Because a parent has more time to spend with her children there is less stress from guilt or worries about child care.

Parents who work full time often worry about the hours spent away from their children. Mothers who stay at home full time often worry about the time lost from a career. Part-time work can help solve both of these problems. By staying involved in your career you can avoid "resume gaps." In addition, by remaining involved in your chosen field, there is a greater chance of exposure to those who will be making future hiring decisions and less chance of technological advances passing you by. There are also the less tangible benefits of having exposure to the outside world and other adults.

Many women begin selling Avon products after talking with an Avon saleswoman and learning about the opportunities available at Avon. Pamela Cook of Charleston, West Virginia, had worried that lack of a college degree as well as her family responsibilities would prevent her from being able to get a job. She began selling Avon products in her home town after her sister, an Avon representative in California, suggested that it might be the solution to Pamela's financial and personal needs. Pamela Cook has flourished in a career that fit her own needs. Says Cook: "Because of what I earn, my quality of life is so much better. My children have benefited in many ways as a result of the additional income. I have a beautiful home and my husband is very proud of me."

The disadvantages of part-time work can be lost income and

benefits and, in some cases, loss of future advancement. Obviously, a family is in an ideal situation if one partner has a job offering solid benefits and salary. The part-time worker is then relieved of the need for a job with health and related benefits. Realistically, there are many of us who do not have this flexibility. If you do, count yourself lucky and think about whether part-time work might help your family get through child-raising with the best combination of time and money.

If part-time work seems to be suitable for you, there are a few pointers worth remembering:

1. If you have a part-time arrangement with your company, *stick to it!* That doesn't mean leaving a meeting early, but it does mean not taking home extra work. Don't commit to an assignment requiring full-time effort on a part-time schedule. You will end up working a full-time job for a part-time salary. That's really stressful.

2. Be prepared for a less-than-enthusiastic response from co-workers—of both sexes. To some extent, part-time employees are threatening to those who would like to work part time, but can't for financial or career reasons. Men and women are equally capable of trying to undermine your decision, just as men and women are equally capable of wanting part-time work. You may be teased about taking it easy or dropping out, and, if you are a man, about wearing the apron strings. The best responses to colleagues' comments are a sense of humor and a strong work ethic. Remind people that you've chosen what's best for you.

3. Be realistic about the possible effects of a part-time stint on your career. If you are determined to become the president of the company, realize that any move to cut back hours may influence promotions and raises. On the other hand, if part-time work allows you the flexibility to be both a happy parent and a fulfilled worker, your overall career may benefit from your personal satisfaction. You might be preparing yourself for

another career pattern. What better person to help a company move into the flexible future than one skilled in the practical application?

4. Don't sell yourself short. Being a part-time worker does not mean that your skills are less valuable. Don't think that since you are *just* part time you are less needed or less important. Be sure to work your assigned hours, and be especially careful to get all work done on time. This is another chance to show your professionalism.

Putting It Together

Most of us will combine many of the options discussed in this and the preceding chapter as we work to balance the emotional, financial, and practical needs and desires of our lives. It is important to see that we do have options. As we've said, and will continue to say throughout the book, people want and need different things. Your goal is to know the things that matter most to you.

Knowing your own priorities is essential to balance. It isn't so important whether you work in a large or small company, full time or part time. What is important is that you know what you want as a result of your working hours and that whatever job you have begin to satisfy those goals.

Things to Remember About Going into Business for Yourself

- In a one-person company, you do everything.
- For many, partnerships allow you great possibilities for balancing life's demands.
- Working with a spouse can strengthen commitment and provide motivation lacking in traditional work situations.
- It is possible, and often advisable, to develop sales skills within the nurturing environment of a company dedicated to training.

- Be realistic when looking at the possibility of working for yourself.
- Part-time work can keep you involved in your career and prevent "resume gaps."

9

Love and Marriage

Just What Are We Talking About When We Say "Love"?

No word is as simple and as complex as "love." At some point we may have thought about the different kinds of love, but chances are, when we think of love what we mean is romantic love. Much of this chapter is going to deal with romantic love, being in love with another person and making a commitment to share our life with that person. In the next chapter, we will also talk about the love we feel for our children and touch on the love we may feel for our communities or our friends.

No emotion has undergone the psychological surgery quite to the same extent as LOVE. We've all had friends become temporarily bitter about love after a disappointment, disillusionment, or divorce. They can't look at or listen to any loving relationship without seeing the flaws. They warn you that whatever behavior your partner is exhibiting was just what their partner was doing before their relationship fell apart. They see tigers behind every bush, infidelity behind every late arrival, an ulterior motive behind every generosity.

To some extent, our society has become a bit like the disenchanted friend—and not without reason. The divorce rate is nearly

50%, the sexual transmission of disease has reached epidemic proportions, and we are constantly being bombarded with books, articles, and magazines that help us measure our love relationship. They tell us how to make it better, stronger, healthier, and more meaningful. We don't have a count of how many articles called "How to Get More Out of Your Relationship" have been published in the last ten years, but we do think the better title might be "What Is the Effect of Your Relationship, or Lack of a Relationship, on the Rest of your Life?" Are you doing and accomplishing in your life the things you want or think you want? How do your relationships support you as an individual? How do your relationships help or hinder you in having balance in your life?

At the same time we are reading divorce statistics, we have all observed and probably experienced firsthand the incredible power of positive love. We've seen men and women blossom under the influence of love. The knowledge and confidence of another's love can provide a cornerstone from which our lives go forth. Having a partner with whom to share a large part of our lives can be wonderful, or at least interesting.

It used to be enough to find a spouse. Now, the pressure is on to have a great relationship. Even though we know that all relationships go through different phases and that some years are better than others, we still put tremendous pressure on ourselves to meet the criteria of others for our relationship. As you read some of our thoughts on today's relationships, try to concentrate on the information that might help you and your partner. If a particular idea doesn't seem in line with what you and your partner want, don't worry about it.

If It Isn't Broke, Don't Fix It

First and foremost, if you are content with your partner, don't submit your relationship to the quizzes and surveys of others. It's important to have confidence in your own patterns and not to worry whether they make any sense to so-called experts. The most important thing for couples to establish is their own "love-style." That doesn't mean that one partner bullies another into a one-sided pattern. If both people are happy with the way their lives interact, if they feel a comfortable balance between their individual personalities and their identity as a part of a couple, there is no reason to subject the relationship to outside judgments.

Another group that has no need to let outside sources influence it is the group made up of happy singles. There are many single people living in the United States today—many of them quite happily. There is no reason to assume that every single person is looking for marriage or even a partner. If you are single and comfortable with your life, including the portion of it concerned with love, relax and enjoy your contentment. Surveys have consistently shown that single women are happier than single men, yet society puts more pressure on women to marry than it does on men. Since women bear the children, this is not hard to understand. At the same time, it is important not to let your feelings be dictated by others.

Most of us probably fall somewhere between being happily married and happily single. Or, we are aware that our feelings may not be the same as several years ago. Perhaps when we married, we had many thoughts about the kind of relationship our marriage would be. The reality of day-to-day life, as well as other changes such as children or the lack of children, may have resulted in a very different kind of marriage from what was first envisioned. The key is whether we can be happy with the relationship we *do* have instead of constantly comparing it to the one we *thought* we would have.

People spend large chunks of their lives being married and single. Our feelings change as we grow older and more confident. For some, the additional confidence (surely one of the strongest advantages of middle age) makes a single life-style less threatening and more attractive. As women begin to increase their earning power, they are better prepared to support themselves financially. Similarly, men and women who once thought of themselves as "confirmed" singles may rather suddenly decide that they want to marry. The point is not to be judgmental about anyone else's life choices. Chances are, you may well find yourself living, and enjoying, something different in the future.

Who Wants Change?

Most of us unhappy with our love lives fall into two categories. There are people dissatisfied with their relationships—relationships that they feel need to be improved if they are going to survive. (For linguistic simplicity, "marriage" and "relationship" shall be used interchangeably.) There are also people looking for a relationship. In that group there are several kinds of singles: those of us who have never married, those of us who are divorced, and those of us whose spouse has died. Each category has a particular effect on exactly how we feel about starting a new relationship.

Even though 50% of marriages end in divorce, there is a growing desire to make marriages last. There seem to be two big influences on the renewed ideal of making marriages last. One is the desire to keep the marriage together for the children. No parents want to hurt their children, and therefore there is renewed effort to try to tackle the problems in a marriage to see if the relationship can be salvaged.

Perhaps even more influential on people trying to work on marriages is the knowledge that many people have found that getting a divorce did not make their lives any better. In fact, divorce usually worsens both partners' financial security. It is more expensive to run two households than one. Both parties may have to find less expensive places to live, thereby disrupting yet another aspect of their lives. Too frequently, men and women divorce and marry someone new, only to find that after the initial infatuation wears off, the new marriage is suffering from many of the same problems as the old marriage. Sadder but wiser, they may make a better effort at saving the second (or third) marriage than they did the first.

Divorce Is Not Always Bad

On the other hand, divorce can be a positive factor for some. Many women (and their children) are physically and/or sexually abused by their husbands. Abusive relationships will not change or go away. The situation will only get worse. Men who batter women will use any excuse to explain their behavior. These very sick men will frequently blame their violence on women——"Dinner wasn't ready," "The house is messy," "It's all your fault." They may apologize profusely after a beating——"I'll never do it again." Without intensive therapy and recognition of the problem, violent men will repeat their behavior. If you are in an abusive relationship or your children are abused, get out. Call a friend or a shelter for battered women. There is help. Many women have been where you are.

You need not be physically abused to be in a dead-end marriage. Staying in a truly unhappy or stifling marriage is not good for anyone. We all have different expectations of marriage. The points of difficulty occur in the gap between your expectations and your reality. Sometimes it's a matter of unrealistic expectations; in other marriages, it's a matter of an unacceptable reality. It isn't always easy to know the difference. If you're troubled about your marriage, talk to someone. Get some perspective on your relationship. Can it be saved? Can it be strengthened? Should it be ended?

Some Ideas on Staying Married

Unfortunately, wanting a marriage to stay together is not enough to make it do so. It takes a tremendous amount of work and compromise, by both partners, to renew and revive a marriage that has fallen into disrepair. But, in the words of the television auto mechanic, "You can pay me now or pay me later." That is, few marriages undergo a period of spontaneous generation once their foundations are endangered. If you think your marriage is in trouble or if you just know that you want more from your marriage, it is important to look at the situation realistically.

Husbands and Wives: The Guide for Men and Women Who Want to Stay Married is written by Drs. Melvin Kinder and Connell Cowan. They believe that many people are unhappy in marriage because they secretly feel their marriage is not measuring up to expectations. The key to their feelings is disillusionment. As Peggy Lee sings, "Is that all there is?" The expectations are not always defined or even really understood by the people who are unhappy. They just have a feeling that there is more, and without really meaning to, they blame their partner for their feelings of not having what they want.

The book explains that marriages are usually made up of two kinds of contracts. The first contract is the one the partners discuss. It usually deals with the issues of fidelity, children, finances (will they both work?) and questions regarding life-style (city or country, own or rent, etc.). The second contract is more secretive and often even unconscious. It is almost never discussed. It deals with what we think our partner will do for us. A common expectation for a woman is that her husband will make her feel whole and give meaning to her life. Men's secret belief is that their wives will give them a happy home life. They secretly think they have married someone who will be a wonderful housekeeper, a perfect mother, and a dynamite sex partner.

As our secret contracts are not fulfilled, our first reaction is to blame someone. Some of us (usually women) blame ourselves. Others blame our partners. A woman who expects marriage and her spouse to give her life definition (certainly a belief our culture has helped form), yet instead finds that she is floundering as an individual, will wonder what is missing from her marriage. Is she a failure or is her husband not giving her enough? Similarly, the man who has an ideal expectation of dinner and lace and happy cherubs will resent (and blame) the woman who can't provide these fantasies of a successful marriage. What both unhappy partners are failing to do is stop and wonder whether their secret contract demands are realistic. Of course, since the demands are at least partly unconscious, it can be tough to get a handle on them. Instead, we have feelings of disillusionment, unhappiness, and anger.

If It Does Need Fixing, What Can We Do?

It's been said before, but it is well worth repeating that *you cannot change another person*. If you feel unhappy in your marriage, the place to start is with yourself, not your spouse. If we spend our time and energy trying to bring about change in our spouse, we are bound to fail. In our mind, their refusal to change is because they do not love us enough. Drs. Kinder and Cowan explain that if you concentrate on working to change yourself, other changes are bound to follow. That is, by changing yourself you change a component in the system of your marriage which is going, in turn, to affect your spouse. We learned in basic science that every action results in a reaction. Apply this technique to marriage. Or at least apply it positively. If you know your partner goes crazy when you leave your clothes on the floor, try picking them up. Similarly, if football is your husband's passion, try learning something about the game.

As we learn to work on our own "secret contract," it is important to try to work on accepting the other person. Newly married people are often surprised that the toothpaste tube debate really does exist. Some people roll the tube up as they go; others seem to thrive on a tube that resembles the Swiss Alps. Whatever your method, it makes more sense to accept your partner's behavior than to end every night waving a tube in the air as proof that he doesn't care for you.

Obviously, marital problems are almost always more serious than the toothpaste debate. But they often begin over small things. And, of course, there are patterns of behavior that you cannot accept. But before you resign yourself to what you think is an unacceptable marriage or find yourself dreaming of a new partner, take some time to try to figure out what is really bugging you. Is it really your partner or is it your disappointment that unknown, unspoken expectations are not being fulfilled?

Marital Myths

You are not alone if you find expectations not being met by marriage. As Drs. Kinder and Cowan explain, every couple has particular beliefs that are harmful to their relationship. Here are some of the more common marital myths.

1. *Marriage will make you feel complete and whole.* This is the number-one unrealistic expectation of marriage. It is also encouraged by everyone around us. If you aren't whole unless

you are married, then marriage must make you whole. Throw away both parts of that equation. Another person cannot solve our personal problems of self-esteem. That doesn't mean that you have to wait until you are perfectly secure before you marry. No one is ever perfectly secure. But it does mean to stop looking to your partner for answers that you must find for yourself.

2. *Your spouse should change for you if she or he really loves you.* As long as you equate change with love, you are setting yourself up for disappointment. The key to love is acceptance. If you hear yourself constantly nagging or correcting, try to figure out what you really want. You may be asking for signs of love, but in a language no one can understand.

3. *If you truly love each other, romance should continue to flourish.* Many of us understand that romance is more about projection than reality. Romance is full of the expectation that this person is *the* person. The problem is dealing with the change from romance to mature love. Afraid of change, we will often try to hold on to romance as security that our spouse still loves us. Romance and love are related but they are not interchangeable. An absence of the romance present in courtship does not mean that there is not love. On the other hand, don't think that because you are married, romance is no longer appropriate.

4. *Your spouse should understand you.* Of course we want a spouse who understands what is important to us. That is part of the process in establishing each family's goals and values. But don't expect your spouse to read your mind.

5. *Differences in need should always be negotiated.* Negotiation is not always good. Sometimes it is important to accept differences rather than continually try to work them out. Differences can be complementary.

6. *In a good marriage, partners have identical dreams and goals.* It is important to establish goals for the family, but don't worry if one of you wants the kids to be rocket scientists while the other wants them to get through high school in one piece.

Accept that you have different feelings because you are each individuals.

7. *A marriage must be stable in order to be healthy.* Stability is a matter for the two of you to work out. Arguments and times of change are going to occur with any people who live together over any length of time.

8. *The more open you are with your mate, the more satisfying your marriage.* Having an open, candid relationship is important. However, privacy is an important element in respecting your spouse. In dealing with your own identity, understand that every detail need not be shared.

9. *If two people are growing individually, it will automatically enhance the marriage.* Don't forget that you got married in order to spend time together. If individual projects are always keeping you apart, the entity that you have as a couple will suffer. It can be difficult to know how to balance individual growth with growth as a couple. If you see that a particular path may be taking you away from your marriage, look at it carefully. Make an effort to talk with your spouse about why you enjoy this particular pursuit.

10. *Sexual disinterest is inevitable in a marriage.* Sexual disinterest is a danger sign that should not be ignored. It is rarely about sex. Sex is a symbolic as well as physical act. It communicates closeness and affection as well as our continued willingness to be vulnerable.

11. *A good marriage should always be fair and equal.* We tend to see behavior that is not like our own as being less fair. We forget that being different is often what attracted us to each other in the first place. Constantly keeping score can damage a relationship. Once again, it is important to try to accept differences.

12. *A woman or a man can be devoted fully to work, family, and marriage.* Nobody can do everything all the time. Learn to work within your own limits and don't expect too much of yourself or your spouse. Establish priorities and work hard to keep all three in balance. On any one day, one may be a higher

priority than the others, but make sure kids and work don't *always* come before marriage.

13. *If you have to "work" on a marriage, something is wrong.* This myth is part of the fairy tale that ends "and they lived happily ever after." We work at getting our spouses and we need to work at keeping them. As we've seen, sometimes "work" is to do nothing. Don't nag, don't analyze, don't keep your marriage under a microscope. On the other hand, do talk about what *you* would like from your marriage, and do work at finding time to spend together.

Once you begin to see how many of these myths may be affecting how you look at your marriage, you may find that letting go of them gives you a lot more operating space. You will also be doing your children a great favor by not creating myths they feel they need to live up to. Many of us grew up in households where myths were prevalent. Even though our own reality may have contradicted the myths, once married, we immediately took them as gospel. You and your spouse are trying to share living and working with each other as each of you goes through life. Don't worry about other people's definitions of what constitutes success or happiness.

How Do We Know
If We Need Help?

OK, the myths have been examined, you see the point, but the problems are not myths. They are real. You really cannot remember what you once felt for each other. Or you do remember, but it's like looking at strangers. Life is short, and yes, you want your marriage to work, but at the same time you are not willing to stay in the situation as it is now. Or, you are worried that if things keep going in the same pattern there will be nothing left to save. What do you do?

Get some help. Talk to your spouse about what you are feeling. Even if things have deteriorated to the point where communication is nearly nil, at least tell him that you have got to find some help. If you can, look for help together. If one partner refuses or is unable to join the search, do it by yourself. Call local community health centers. Talk to your minister, priest, or rabbi. See if local bookstores have books by professionals in the community. Ask your friends if they have recommendations. You might think that it is hard to tell friends that you need some guidance, and it may be; but chances are your friends have been there too. One of the best ways to dispel some myths is to find out that the "perfect" marriage down the street nearly fell apart a few years back. *Every marriage has times of difficulty.* The difference in couples is what they do about it.

Things to Remember About Love and Marriage

- At the same time we are reading divorce statistics, we have all observed and probably experienced firsthand the incredible power of positive love.
- If you are content with your partner, don't submit your relationship to the quizzes and surveys of others.
- Can you be happy with the relationship you *do* have instead of constantly comparing it to the one you *thought* you would have?
- Divorce can be a positive factor for some. Staying in a truly unhappy or stifling marriage is not good for anyone.
- Concentrate on working to change yourself; other changes are bound to follow.
- Don't worry about other people's definitions of what constitutes success or happiness.

10

Love and Friendship

Single people who have read about marriage myths may decide that staying single is not such a bad option. However, single people have myths too. It is easy to put a life on hold, waiting for that one person who will make all the daily problems of work and life so much easier. Even if we were married before, we might still harbor the thought that "*this time* I won't make a mistake."

Looking for Love

We can't and therefore won't try to tell you a sure-fire method for finding love, but we do have some ideas about finding a balance between being a confident single person and being a man or woman interested in meeting a special person. It is possible to be single, happy, and interested in meeting a partner all at the same time.

Now that we all know marriage cannot provide us with emotional well-being, that we must find this for ourselves; there is no need to put pressure on ourselves to find instant love. Instead of looking for love, try making the commitment to meet new people and work on developing friendships. It is much easier to meet and get acquainted with people if we are not craning our necks looking for Mr. or Ms. "right" to the exclusion of the person standing in front of us.

It is fun to look for people with whom you would like to be friends. Besides taking the pressure off yourself to find true love, you will give yourself a chance to learn about your own behavior. Watch yourself as you are introduced to people. Are you equally friendly or receptive regardless of the situation, or do you find yourself nervous and awkward if you know the stranger is a potential date? Are you friendlier to the person who appears to be financially well off, or do you find yourself drawn to those who seem to need your help? The more you learn to pay attention to your own personal patterns, the better you can identify your friendship behavior.

Most of us learned how to make friends when we were children. We would meet at school or in the neighborhood, and after a few pertinent questions such as "How old are you?," "Where do you live?," and "What toys do you have?," a vague decision regarding being friends was established. There were some kids we liked immediately and others we disliked just as quickly. With little or no conscious thought, relationships were formed and loyalties established. The pattern remains pretty much the same as we grow older, with fewer direct questions about toys and more about "What do you do?" At some point, especially if we are trying to make friends of the opposite sex, it is important to assume those friendship behaviors we established as children. Take the pressure off yourself; you're meeting a potential new friend, not a potential husband or wife.

If your goal in meeting people is friendship instead of love, you have a much better chance of success. Few of us consider calling someone a friend after one lunch. Yet we have all had at least one experience of being in love after one date. We called it love because we wanted it to be love. Even if you know that what you want is love, try working on friendship instead. The two are not mutually exclusive: the elements of friendship such as trust and respect are vital parts of loving someone.

Some Further Thoughts on Meeting People

The Office—Friend or Foe?

Work is a natural environment for men and women to meet. Many people meet their spouses through work. Sometimes it is someone in the office, and frequently it's an introduction via a colleague. It is important to understand that there might be pitfalls in falling for a colleague. There's a risk of upsetting the balance between work and pleasure when we date a co-worker. There is also the problem of a romance upsetting the existing balance between a group of co-workers.

If we were to describe the perfect office romance it would be between two single people, working in different departments, with absolutely no authority over each other's performance or salary. That description should give you an idea of some typical difficulties romantic colleagues can run into.

First and foremost, the only thing worse than having an affair or romance with a married person is having this adulterous affair with someone in your office. It doesn't work. It undermines the respect of your colleagues (no secret is ever *really* secret in an office), has the potential to damage your personal and professional reputation, and makes a huge mess when the affair is over. Any momentary thrills are tremendously overshadowed by all the things you have to lose.

If you are both single, the situation improves. Now the chief problems have to do with the way you relate to each other at work and potential accusations of favoritism. Office affairs frequently involve people who work closely together. They get to know each other on joint projects and spend a lot of time with each other. It is not unusual for one person to have management authority over the other. Once again, this can be tremendously upsetting to colleagues, who may realistically worry about favoritism. The manager's authority suffers, and the subordinate may not receive the proper recognition for being a talented worker. If you really are in love, you might want to consider changing jobs or asking for a transfer to another department.

Age Discrimination and Dating

No, you can't be sued for refusing to date someone because of their age, but you *can* be missing out on a lot of fun. Women get sick of personal ads placed by men nearly always wanting a woman at least five years younger. At the same time, women are often uneasy about dating men who are younger than they are. Try waiting to see how you feel about someone before quizzing them about their age.

Don't be taken aback if you find yourself attracted to someone younger or older. There are few rules here (though it can be tough if either party is near the age of your children) and often very good reasons for pursuing a relationship that once you might not have considered.

That's What Friends Are For

We've said that an important element of love is friendship. Friendship is also a critical element in balance. Our friends are an important support system in today's busy and often conflicting world. Our friends offer consistency and commitment. They are often a link to parts of our past and people with whom we can share a vision of what we want in the future.

It is often difficult to find the time to keep up with friends. Often we are not living in the same town, or our friends have equally busy lives. It often seems impossible to juggle two schedules and find some time to spend together. Once again, the key is knowing that the friendship is important to you and then making the commitment to give it some time.

Low-Maintenance Friends

A married working mother of three talks about the need for today's women to have "low-maintenance" friendships. What she means is that she doesn't have time to be a perfect friend—she may forget a birthday, not call every week, or take a couple of days to call back. She needs her friends to trust that her affection and caring are there, but that she can't "be there" every day. These days it is difficult to have a demanding friend.

The same woman has several traditions with her friends that help hold the relationships together throughout the year. She has a simple open house every year before Christmas, which always includes old friends as well as new. At least twice a year there are "girls night out" evenings which give friends a chance to have dinner without husbands or children. And, when some unexpected time opens up, she usually calls a friend first.

This ability to have friends without being in constant touch works best when there is an agreement that in times of trouble or great success a friend should be clear and specific about her need for her friend. True friendships do not rely on mind reading. If you have a problem and need your friend, tell her. If you have a promotion or accolade to share, let her know. Don't put your friends in the position of not knowing something because you didn't tell them.

The Relationship Between Guilt and Love

Do you feel guilty a lot? If you are a criminal, then your guilt may be appropriate, but if you are an honest individual—married or single —love may be at the root of your guilt. When we love someone we place expectations on our behavior toward that person. We think, often without realizing it, that if we loved them we would do _____ (fill in the blank). When we disappoint ourselves by being unable to always follow through on our idealized expectations, we feel guilty.

Sometimes we feel stretched to the limit because we're suffering from too much love. We may feel very strongly about many people and end up feeling that we are selling them short because we are unable to give each of them the time, or love, that we think is required. If you're worried that you are letting someone down, say something. At the same time, keep your expectations realistic.

In order to achieve balance, we've got to get our expectations in line with what is really possible. If you are a mother with a full-time job outside the home, you cannot pick your child up at school every day. You can either learn to accept that reality or you can feel guilty about it every day at three o'clock. Guilt is not an appropriate substitute for love. Forgiveness is much closer to love than guilt. Forgive yourself and forgive those around you.

In *Guilt Is the Teacher, Love Is the Lesson,* Boston psychotherapist Joan Borysenko lists four signs of unhealthy guilt. They are:

1. *Being overcommitted.* You have too many projects, too much to do.
2. *You have no time for yourself.* You are last on your priority list.
3. *Perfectionism.* You feel the desire to be perfect as an emotional need, not an intellectual choice.
4. *You feel selfish.* You are often angry at those you spend so much time helping because it leaves so little time and energy for you; then you secretly worry that you may be selfish.

On a given day, we all have some of these symptoms. If you realize that you have all of them *all* the time, you might want to go back and reread the section on taking control of your life.

Women used to corner the market on guilt, but now men are beginning to suffer from guilt when their jobs and home demands and desires are in conflict. As more men want to have a bigger part in raising their children, they feel guilty when they don't. If you see you are feeling guilty because you're not able to do it all, take a little time to assess realistically what you *can* do for those you love.

Loving Your Children— When Is It Too Much?

Next to our spouses, most of our loving goes to our children. From the time when they are helpless and need us for survival to the time when we can enjoy their triumphs as independent adults, we are bound up in their lives. Many of us feel that there is nothing we wouldn't do for our children, yet sometimes it is that propensity to do it all for them that gets us and them into trouble.

We all learn from our mistakes. We need to allow our children enough room to make mistakes while still letting them know we are there for support and guidance. If you find yourself staying up all night to write a history report for a seventh-grader, you are probably doing too much for your child. Children need to learn that they *can* do it without you. They also need to learn the consequences of not doing their homework. Try to think about the times you need to be close to your children and the times you need to stay out of their lives. It's a delicate balance, and the only sure answer is that it shouldn't be all or nothing.

Throughout this book, we have discussed the many different ways to try to achieve a balance between the many responsibilities and joys in our lives. Our families, jobs, and communities need us and we need them. Too often we forget why and how we got ourselves into these busy lives in the first place. An argument could be made that at the root of all endeavors is love.

We cannot examine all the different ways love motivates us, but it is important to remember that caring for someone or something is frequently behind our involvement. Sometimes the connection is direct, as in marriage. At other times the connection might be less obvious. The motivation behind many political and environmental activists is the desire to leave the world a "better place." The love of children is a powerful force. We may also love our work (and the money our work provides). Love is not only romantic. Love is powerful and it is rewarding. Often it is not an end in itself, but a means to an end—happiness, a better future, a life in balance. As a closing comment on love, remember that actions speak louder than words.

Things to Remember About Love

- Don't put your life on hold, waiting for that one person you think will make life easier.
- It is fun to look for people with whom you would like to be friends.
- Understand the positives and the negatives of office romances.
- Friendships that form and last over a period of time can be rewarding and positive relationships as we look for love.

- In order to achieve balance, you've got to get your expectations in line with what is really possible.
- Loving your children doesn't mean that you do everything for them.

11

Health and Fitness

As discussed throughout the book, dual-career couples with children are challenged to be their best every day. In order to enjoy these busy lives, it is very important to feel good. It is also essential that we be in good physical shape in order to have the stamina needed for these diverse lives. Luckily, feeling good and being physically fit are not mutually exclusive, but rather different sides of the same coin. If your body is in good shape and working efficiently, it will show in the way you look and feel. When you are happy with yourself you will have more energy. In turn, this energy will inspire you to get more exercise and therefore continue looking and feeling good.

Conversely, when we don't feel good it is harder to motivate ourselves. We all know how uncomfortable a tight waistband can be. Trying to live our busy lives without taking care of ourselves is a bit like having a tight waistband all the time. We feel we have too much to do and no way to get it done. We are not comfortable. Life is overwhelming, not challenging. We drink coffee and eat donuts for energy, we sit in order to become rested, and we choose alcohol and/or drugs for relaxation and stress relief. It is hard to imagine how to change this treadmill. You've got to trust the experts and the studies. You will enjoy your life more if you improve your health.

Throughout this book we have discussed the ways in which men and women can learn to balance their lives. Whether at work or at home, it's important to know that your actions matter. Perhaps the most important message is that an active approach to life is the key to getting what you want. Set goals, take control, make changes, communicate, believe. Understand that the life you are now living is not a dress rehearsal for the real thing. This is it, and it's a lot more fun and fulfilling to be a participant rather than a spectator. There is another, quite literal, way that this active approach to balance can be utilized—exercise.

The Importance and Benefits of Regular Exercise

Regular exercise provides several benefits that help achieve a balanced life. Recent research has shown that exercise is a major factor in building stamina. Aerobic exercise increases the amount of oxygen in the bloodstream, which in turn increases our energy. Instead of thinking you are too tired to exercise, you may be tired because you are not getting enough exercise. Instead of napping 30 minutes a day, try substituting a brisk walk. As your stamina increases you will see that you are accomplishing more during the day.

In addition to building stamina, exercise also helps reduce stress in our lives. Stress is a natural result of a demanding life. It is also an obstacle in achieving balance. It is harder to make decisions under stress. It is also more difficult to work efficiently and enjoyably if you feel as though you are under the same amount of pressure as Ivan Lendl's tennis racket. Exercise helps control and reduce stress in at least two ways. First, exercise produces beta-endorphins, which are shown to increase our sense of well-being. While walking two or three miles a day may not give you a "runner's high," it will clear your head and improve your mood. Secondly, well-conditioned bodies respond best to stressful situations. They produce less adrenaline and so keep the heart from racing. Regular exercise conditions your body to stress, which improves the response to nonexercise-induced stress. We've all seen the ways different people respond to emergencies. The calm, assured response inspires confidence and helps everyone work better.

Another benefit of regular exercise is improved creativity. A study at Baruch College tested students on creative problem-solving before and after 20 minutes of exercise. They performed much better after the exercise. It was easier for them to solve problems after following a regular program of exercise. It is believed that exercise helps our thinking by changing the brain-wave patterns. More alpha waves are produced during exercise. This means that we are tapping into the right side of our brain, generally thought to be the "intuitive" side of the brain, as opposed to the left or "analytic" side. By exercising, we are helping ourselves find a new way of seeing something. It's easy to see that improved thinking and problem-solving are keys to balance.

How Much Exercise and Establishing a Routine

It doesn't take hours to achieve the results discussed above. You don't have to be able to run a marathon in order to be in shape. Many people don't develop a regular exercise program because they think they don't have enough time to work out. It is not necessarily true that more exercise makes you healthier. The Institute for Aerobics Research in Dallas recommends achieving moderate fitness by walking two miles in less than 30 minutes at least three days a week or walking two miles in 30–40 minutes five or six times a week. For higher fitness, the minimum suggested is walking two miles in less than 30 minutes five or six days a week or running two miles in 20–24 minutes four days a week. Many people make exercise a much bigger part of their lives, which is great, but don't feel you have to invest large amounts of time or money in order to achieve big benefits.

To help maintain a regular exercise schedule, try following some of these guidelines:

1. Put exercise at the top of your to-do list at least four times a week. Don't schedule four days on followed by three days off.

Benefits are greatest when days of exercise and rest are interspersed. Most experts recommend at least one day a week off to give your body a chance to recover and prevent injury.

2. Exercise in the morning. Like most activities, the ones we schedule to do first have the greatest chance of getting done. In addition, a morning walk or ride (stationary or real bicycle) is a great time to think about the workday ahead. As discussed, your brain is working well in the morning and you are likely to see solutions that were not apparent the day before.

3. Don't overcommit at the beginning. Too much exercise before your body is conditioned may lead to injury. If injured, you can't exercise and you've burdened your already complex day with another handicap.

4. If your job requires a lot of travel, don't let it interfere with your schedule. Many hotels have gyms and/or pools. Make sure your corporate travel department or assistant knows your preferences. In addition, more and more health clubs have reciprocal arrangements with clubs in other cities. If you travel frequently, you might want to investigate this service before spending a lot of money on a membership.

5. If you exercise outdoors, it is usually a good idea to have a backup in case the weather is bad. Also, people who complain that exercise is boring may find it more fun to alternate their routine. Change your route if you walk or run. If you ride a stationary cycle, try listening to upbeat music to break the monotony. Others save pleasure reading for the stationary bike. If you are reading a particularly good chapter you may find that you are extending your workout with no extra effort.

Diet

Diet, like exercise, is a boon to improving your stamina as well as the way you look and feel. Unfortunately, the word "diet" is too often associated with deprivation and guilt as opposed to nourishment and health. Instead of thinking of diet as a verb, something you "go on," try thinking of diet as a noun. Your diet is what you eat every day. As more and more people realize that eating healthy is one of the simplest ways to look good, feel great, and live longer, we can begin to see food as an ally rather than an enemy.

Another reason to banish the diet verb from our life is that dieting to lose weight provides a short-term solution to a long-term concern. It is estimated that 75%–90% of the people who lose weight regain it. Of those who lose over 40 pounds, 95% regain the weight within two years. To make matters worse, those who take off weight quickly often regain more than they originally lost. There are no quick solutions to weight loss. There are slower methods that greatly improve your chances of permanent rather than temporary changes. If you do want to lose weight, don't think of it as a temporary phase of your life. You didn't gain the excess weight in two weeks, so don't try to lose it all at once. Think of making permanent changes rather than temporary ones.

Think of diet as an overall plan to help the way you look and feel. Your daily choices over the course of a year are much more important than what you do for two weeks. Also, be honest about the way you look. Don't be unrealistic about your expectations. In general, society is much more accepting of a range of sizes for men than it is for women. If becoming a size eight is going to mean never eating what you enjoy, is it worth it? Look around at your friends and colleagues. What makes you admire some more than others? Surely it is not their dress size that's most important to you.

Whether your goal is to lose weight or not, the combination of an everyday healthy diet and regular exercise will do wonders for the way you look and feel. There is no one diet that will suit everyone's needs and also please everyone's taste buds. However, the American Cancer Society does have suggested guidelines which everyone can use. They are:

1. Eat more high-fiber foods such as fruits, vegetables, and whole-grain cereals.

2. Include dark green and deep yellow fruits and vegetables rich in vitamins A and C.

3. Include cabbage, broccoli, brussels sprouts, and cauliflower.

4. Be moderate in consumption of salt-cured, smoked, and nitrate-cured foods.

5. Cut down on total fat intake from animal sources and other fats and oils.

6. Be moderate in consumption of alcoholic beverages.

Note the words "moderate" and "cut down." A healthy diet doesn't mean that you can never eat creamy pasta with bacon again. It means that you should make it an exception rather than the rule. Follow the commonsense approach to eating. Think in terms of cutting back on rich foods and increasing leafy greens instead of thinking that "rabbit food" is all you can eat. Obviously, those of us with serious health problems influenced by diet such as diabetes or high cholesterol need to be more selective about our daily choices. If you do have specific health concerns, be sure to talk with your doctor or nutritionist about the best diet for you.

PMS—Premenstrual Syndrome

Four out of five women experience some degree of premenstrual syndrome. Symptoms vary with the individual but most common are feelings of bloating, irritability, depression, and changes in appetite sometime during the two weeks preceding their period. No one knows exactly what causes PMS, but there are some indications that hormonal changes are a part of the cause. For some women, the problems are relatively minor and infrequent. For others they occur *every* month and can be quite severe. In addition to talking with your doctor, there are some simple things you can do to try to lessen the severity of PMS.

1. Eat a high-carbohydrate, low-protein diet. This was shown to help over 50% of the women in a study at the Massachusetts Institute of Technology.

2. Cutting back on salt, especially before the onset of PMS, helps many women reduce symptoms of bloating. Also, drinking lots of water helps cleanse your system, and it doesn't increase puffiness.

3. Aerobic exercise helps with depression and fatigue. Try to exercise before symptoms start.

Keep track of your cycle and be aware of potential bad days. Talk with your doctor, watch your diet, keep exercising, and hope you don't yell at the wrong person.

Sleep

Food is not the only healthy thing people are being too stingy with today. One way many people have tried to achieve balance is by cutting back on their sleep. With so many things to do and a finite number of hours in the day, it has become necessary for people to cut an hour or two of sleep a night in order to get everything done. Unfortunately, this "solution" is not an answer at all, but instead the beginning of a serious problem. Dr. Charles Pollack, head of the sleep disorders unit at Cornell University's New York Hospital in Westchester, New York, believes that sleepiness is one of the least-recognized sources of disability in our society.

People who don't get enough sleep are unable to think clearly. Their judgment is poor and they are unable to sustain a long attention span. By cutting back on sleep, you may be making your work harder and your day longer by not being able to work efficiently. Studies show that even two nights of inadequate sleep results in a drop in the ability to do rote functioning such as adding columns of numbers or pressing the right button. In our highly technological society these problems in functioning can have severe consequences.

It is estimated that drowsiness causes 60%–90% of all workplace accidents. The largest number of these accidents occur on the late-night shift, where workers are under a severe sleep handicap. Over 200,000 automobile accidents a year are caused by sleep-deprived drivers. An increased awareness of mistakes made by exhausted medical interns and residents has resulted in new thinking on the maximum number of hours a doctor should be allowed to be on call.

Another result of lack of sleep is irritability and crankiness. Our tempers flare more easily when we are tired, which only adds to the existing stress. We all know that a sleepy child is not at his or her best. The same is true for teens and adults. Our families and co-workers suffer from our lack of sleep, even though few of us accept that sleep is the valuable commodity research is proving it to be. Rather than being at the end of our list of priorities, sufficient sleep needs to be placed near the top of the list. Without enough sleep, it is nearly impossible to implement a plan for balance.

How Much Sleep Do You Need?

We all know the individual dynamos of success who need only four to five hours of sleep a night. Margaret Thatcher, former prime minister of Great Britain, feels strongly that one factor in her rise to the top of the British Government was that she rarely required over five hours of sleep a night. At the other end of the spectrum are people who swear by 10 to 12 hours of sleep per night. Comedian, writer, and creative genius Steve Allen has stated that he requires a minimum of 12 hours of sleep a night in order to function at his best. Most of us fall in between these two extremes.

While experts believe that most adults need eight hours of sleep a night in order to function at their best, many of us laugh at the notion of trying to get that much sleep a night. How can it be done? For many, the answer is to go to bed earlier. Instead of the late news, which often leads to the late movie, more people are turning off the TV set and the lights and going to bed shortly after the children are asleep. More people are unplugging their telephones at night or turning down the volume on the answering machine and sleeping through late-night messages. Tell your friends not to call after a certain hour. Learning to say no to outside interruptions and yes to more sleep will help you find balance.

Going to bed early is not such a revolutionary thought. It's how all humans responded before electric lights. The sun was the guide for the beginning and end of the workday. There were no all-night restaurants, grocery stores, or graveyard shifts. The problem for many of us is we feel almost forced to take advantage of our round-the-clock society. With the lack of outer limits, many of us have failed to establish our own limits. In the '80s, it was frequently a sign of success and power to proclaim how little sleep you needed. After an exhausting decade, people are beginning to realize that the overall quality of their lives begins with being well rested.

Sleep and Marriage

A recent experiment at Brigham Young University by marriage counselor and family therapist Jeffrey Larson, Ph.D., showed that couples who go to bed and get up together have happier marriages. Studying 150 couples, 94% of those whose sleep patterns and rhythms were in sync said that they had happy marriages. On the other hand, over one-third of the couples whose sleep patterns were independent of each other reported more fighting, less sex, and generally less happy marriages. So try going to bed earlier with your spouse. If your patterns are really different—a night owl and an early bird, for example—try adjusting to each other's cycle. See if you can find an alternating pattern that allows you to begin and end the majority of your days together. People's sleep patterns and natural rhythms aren't whims. If your spouse really has to stay up until two, don't take it personally. Do try to see if both of you can be flexible occasionally. Sleeping together, with or without sex, is a wonderful way to re-establish and/or maintain intimacy.

Body and Soul

We have discussed the need to keep our bodies in shape. The combination of regular exercise (remember, walking can be exercise!) and a balanced diet will improve the way you look and feel and help control and reduce stress. A healthy body is also a key to stamina—the ability to get through days with vitality and vigor instead of frustration and exhaustion.

A healthy body is also an indicator that you feel good about yourself. The mind-body relationship is a little like debating which came first, the chicken or the egg. What we do know is that people who think positively about themselves and their bodies are healthier than people who are pessimistic. Changing the way we think, especially the way we think about ourselves, is not an overnight change. Neither is it a huge undertaking. Try setting a particular time each day to think great things about yourself. Learn to picture yourself accomplishing one of your big goals. If you've started a walking program, try combining the two. You'll already be feeling positive because you are exercising. Another time to give yourself a boost of positive thinking is before you go to sleep. Spend a few minutes daydreaming as you go to sleep.

In addition to mind and body, there is also a nonquantitative body part that needs to be cared for and nurtured. We call it spirit. More than anything else, spirit helps us find the desire and energy to go on in an ever-complex world. There are a lot of bad things in the world: Poverty, crime, pollution, drugs and disease are in every community. It's easy for the overwhelming problems to discourage us. They also alienate us by shadowing the importance of individual efforts. It's easy to feel helpless as we face the things that frighten and threaten us. To some extent this is depression on a national level. We often hide our fear and frustration behind cynicism and sarcasm. It's hard to bound out of bed with energy and commitment when the newspaper and morning news remind us of all the uphill battles out there. It's especially hard if we went to bed demoralized the night before. The very nature of today's world makes it especially important that we make every effort—mentally, physically, and spiritually—to combat the hazards.

More than anything else, spirit may be making a commitment to accepting your place in the world and becoming a part of it instead of just being an observer. Spirit is accepting—perhaps even enthusiastically accepting—that we are human and part of the human history of our time. Spirit is made up of attachments. To be balanced we need attachments outside ourselves. Our children help give us a sense of future. Our community can help us find a sense of order and purpose in our daily lives. Poverty seems a little less devastating if we've worked on a food drive, pollution less threatening if we've recycled most of our garbage. A key to feeling good is empowerment. You can quit smoking, you can drink less, you can walk two miles three times a week, you can take small steps and make a long journey. The journey is living a full life every day. The small steps are learning to feel good about yourself, physically, mentally, and spiritually.

Things to Remember About Health and Fitness

- Good health is a key to balance.
- Regular exercise helps control weight, reduce stress, improve thinking, and increase energy.
- Try to get off the diet treadmill. Think of diet as daily choices.
- One of the best things you can do for balance is to get more sleep.
- Be aware of the relationship between mind and body.

12

Signs of the Times— Health Problems

Depression

Few words are used in contemporary American society as frequently as "depression." It punctuates our speech as an adverb or adjective. Does the word describe a particular mood or malaise or is it a catch-all word to explain why we don't get things done? Most of us grew up knowing little about depression. We were told to "buck up" when we were sad. We were not encouraged to explore our emotions. What exactly is depression? We know that depression is a major problem for men and women in the 1990s. Studies show that women are twice as likely to suffer from depression as men. Whether you are a man or woman, depression is not an unimportant health issue. When we are depressed, we work poorly, get sick more often, and have little to offer those around us. In all likelihood, we will all have at least one encounter with depression; if not personally, then through someone with whom we live or work.

More and more frequently we see the word "depression" used to describe an illness. It is usually preceded by the words "suffer from."

We know what it means to suffer from a headache, we know what it means to suffer from the flu, but what does it mean to suffer from depression? A start to understanding the nature of depression may be found in the criteria listed in the *Diagnostic and Statistical Manual of the American Psychiatric Association*. The guidelines suggest that anyone suffering from five of the following nine symptoms is suffering from a major depressive episode.

1. Depressed mood
2. Loss of interest in usual activities
3. Loss of appetite
4. Insomnia
5. Psychomotor retardation (slow thought or movement)
6. Loss of energy
7. Feelings of worthlessness or guilt
8. Diminished ability to think or poor concentration
9. Suicidal thought or action

Is depression ever normal? Does depression always require therapy or drugs in order to go away? What's the difference between the rainy-day blues and the beginnings of a serious long-lasting depression? There are no simple answers to these questions. Experts disagree on the causes and the cures of depression. In addition to the number of symptoms, it is important to take into account how long the symptoms have been present. Many of us have bad days; it is more serious when we realize we've had a bad week or two. It is clear that depression is a serious health problem of the '90s.

Most of us know to call a doctor when we have a fever or are in physical pain. Unfortunately, depression is not as obvious, or we may not feel that we should seek help for symptoms that lack the clarity or physical manifestation of the flu. Perhaps the most insidious aspect of depression is that it makes it difficult to seek help from friends or doctors when we most need it. Because depression is frequently accompanied by feelings of worthlessness, it is hard for us to understand that we are able to, as well as deserve to, get help.

No one knows exactly what causes depression, and there is no real agreement on treatment. Some experts feel that depression is a result of "anger turned inward" and might suggest psychotherapy as the primary treatment. Others feel that depression is primarily chemical in nature and, therefore, are strong advocates for drug therapy. Another theory on the cause of depression now coming to the forefront seems to offer both an explanation and a relatively simple cure or preventive measure. The theory is that our feelings are a direct result of our thinking. If we think pessimistically, we will be more likely to be depressed, whereas if we think optimistically, we will lessen the chance as well as the severity of depression. These ideas are discussed in great detail in *Learned Optimism* by Martin Seligman, Ph.D.

One of Dr. Seligman's themes is that someone who has a pessimistic explanatory style is more likely to become depressed than one who learns to explain events in a more optimistic matter. Bad things happen to good people all the time. By bad we mean something that we wish had not happened. It can be as simple as not getting the garbage out on time for pickup or more serious such as getting turned down for a raise. What we say to ourselves when we do not get what we want is very important. Dr. Seligman uses the words *personal, permanent,* and *pervasive* to help us examine the way we think. When something bad happens, do you:

1. Take it *personally:* "I didn't get the raise because I'm not good enough."
2. Make *permanent* conclusions: "I'll never make more money."
3. Apply these thoughts *pervasively* to your life: "I'm no good at anything and will just keep failing no matter what I do."

What if we could learn to change those thoughts to:

1. Nonpersonal: "They aren't giving raises."
2. Temporary as opposed to permanent: "Raises are hard to come by this year."
3. Singular rather than pervasive: "This is a disappointment in one part of my life."

If our outlook and personal interpretation are always negative or pessimistic, it makes sense that we will be more prone to depression. Our thoughts have direct effects on our feelings. Our thoughts are also reinforcing. If you think negatively about yourself, you are more likely to accept your failures. On the other hand, if you think positively, you are more likely to believe that your hard work will pay off. This belief in our own ability to do things well is often the key to finding the energy for the extra effort required for a job well done.

Why Women?

Women are twice as likely as men to become depressed. While it's difficult to know what is caused by nature—inborn—and what is caused by nurture—taught to women as they develop—it is clear that women are more likely to think that their failures are the direct result of their actions. Women are quick to take too much responsibility for failures. As women's lives have become more demanding, with many having or choosing to work outside the home, few have allowed themselves to accept that they can't do everything. Coupled with their own unrealistic expectations are their tendencies to blame themselves for any result that is less than perfect. It's important that women learn to think more positively about their actions and be more realistic about their expectations.

Women can learn a lot about taking less responsibility for things out of their control by listening to men. Men just don't worry so much that they *should* have known better. For example: If a man misses a meeting because of an accident on the highway, he might say, "Some jerk had a wreck, sorry." A woman's response might be "There was a terrible accident. I should have left earlier or known to take the other road. Can you forgive me?" The best advice for women might be to cut their thoughts off quicker. Don't take so much responsibility. Let accidents happen.

Helping Those Around You

Negative thinking is often encouraged by those around us. If a child hears parents having personal, permanent, and pervasive thoughts about their actions, the child will pick up the same reasoning. Listen to yourself and your children in the daily setbacks natural to life.

Work with your children to help them see that failure is temporary and that a particular failure is only one aspect of their lives. Work with them to overcome negative thinking. Listen for pessimistic thinking among your co-workers and subordinates. A good manager needs to motivate as well as supervise. If you hear negative reasoning, take the time to talk to the employee. Build her confidence by reminding her about past successes. Take a minute and think about how you criticize those around you. Do not use words like "always" or "never." Try to change your comments to include temporary words, for example: "I was disappointed in your report at the meeting last week" instead of "Your reports are never very good and you always let me down." If you hear yourself being tough on your colleagues, take a few minutes and consider the way you judge yourself. Most people who are hard on others are even harder on themselves.

Addictions and Dependencies

Perhaps another indication of the amount of unhappiness in our society is that there are 30 million alcohol and drug addicts, affecting one in three American families. Once again, at work or at home, all of us are affected by these problems. What constitutes a chemical dependency? A good definition is found in *Dare to Confront!* by Bob Wright and Deborah George Wright:

> Chemical dependency is a physical, mental, and/or emotional need for a mind-altering substance where continued use takes precedence over family, friends, co-workers, job, health, the law, or financial stability.

If people with whom we live or work put their need for drugs or alcohol above everything else, they are jeopardizing our well-being as well as their own. It isn't just their problem. We can all recognize that a drunk driver threatens everyone on the road. It's more difficult to recognize the threat to our jobs and family when the evidence is less clear. Don't be afraid to recognize signs of chemical dependency around you. Answering the following questions from *Dare to Con-*

front! can help you assess whether a loved one, friend, co-worker, or yourself has a chemical dependency problem:

1. Has this person's drinking or using drugs ever caused you embarrassment?

2. Does this person's drinking or using drugs make the atmosphere uncomfortable and tense?

3. Has this person ever had a loss of memory as a result of drinking or using drugs?

4. Are you concerned about this person's association with other heavy drinkers or drug users?

5. Has this person made and broken numerous promises to stop drinking or using drugs?

6. Does this person expect you to lie and make excuses to cover up his/her drinking or using drugs?

7. Has this person's use of alcohol or drugs caused difficulty on the job, at home, or socially?

8. Has this person's drinking or using drugs ever caused a medical, legal, or financial problem?

9. Is this person's drinking or using drugs affecting his or her reputation?

10. Has anyone outside the family ever expressed concern about this person's use of alcohol or drugs?

11. Does this person consider holidays, weekends, and special events as drinking or drugging celebrations?

12. Does this person use drink or drugs in response to good news and bad news?

13. Do you or others get upset or uneasy when this person is present?

14. Does this person refuse to allow discussions of his or her drinking or drug using?

15. Do you feel that, if pushed, this person would choose the chemical over continuing the relationship?

16. When under the influence of alcohol or drug, does this person drive a car?

17. Does this person drink or use drugs to build self-confidence?

18. Does this person often try to rationalize or explain away the need for alcohol or drugs?
19. Does this person keep a ready supply of alcohol and drugs hidden away from others in peculiar places?
20. Does this person regularly frequent places where alcohol or drugs are heavily used?

Five or more "yes" answers may indicate a problem and you may want to consult a professional.

If There Is a Problem

Perhaps the most important things to know about a problem in ourselves or others are that it won't go away by itself and that there are many avenues for seeking help. The only good thing to come out of our current epidemic of drug and alcohol abuse is that we have learned that these problems can happen to anyone—men and women, rich and poor, messengers and moguls. No one is free from risk; neither is anyone alone.

There are many groups available to help the chemically dependent person as well as those affected by his or her behavior. If you think you or someone in your life has a serious problem, seek out information. Your church or community center will be able to give you names of organizations set up to help you. Go to a bookstore and look through the self-help section. You might be surprised at the number of books available to help you find solutions. Most books will contain a list of references and groups. The key is not to ignore the problem. Take control of the situation, but don't think you have to do it alone.

Eating Disorders

It is important to be aware of eating disorders, especially if you are a mother or work with preteen and teenage girls. Boys and men also suffer from eating disorders but not with the frequency of girls and women. The most common eating disorders are *Anorexia Nervosa* and *Bulimia*. Anorexia nervosa is most common in preteens and teenagers, while bulimia usually begins at about age eighteen. With anorexia nervosa, young people quit eating as a result of a distorted self-image. They feel "fat" even though they may be severely underweight. They are often high achievers with an unrealistic desire for perfection. If not treated, anorexia nervosa can result in death by starvation. Some signs to look for are: your daughter never eating in front of you, always saying she "already ate," being obsessed with weight, and looking too thin.

Bulimia is a system of binging and purging. That is, the person with bulimia will vomit shortly after eating large quantities of food. She may also rely on laxatives to purge her body of food. Signs to look for are: spending an unusual amount of time in the bathroom, the regular consumption of large quantities of food, and never gaining weight. Untreated bulimia can also result in death. The constant vomiting robs the body of nutrition and disrupts the entire body's chemical balance. There can also be significant tooth destruction as a result of the acids in the mouth.

These disorders are not unusual and they are treatable. There are doctors and clinics specializing in eating disorders. In addition, there is a heightened awareness among schoolteachers and family doctors about the problems and symptoms of these disorders. If you are worried about someone, talk to her. If you can, get her to a doctor for a checkup. Information is out there—use it.

A Word on Smoking

In case you missed it, when C. Everett Koop was Surgeon General of the United States, he stated that the most addictive substance in our society is nicotine. Rather than be discouraged by this news (smokers already know it), take heart in the success millions of Americans have had kicking the habit. *It's never too late* to quit smoking. It seems certain that anyone still smoking must know the huge risks to their health and the health of those around them. Quitting smoking is hard, but those who have done it are buoyed by the knowledge that they conquered their addiction. Many say they can draw on the fortitude and self-control they used to quit smoking to inspire them as they take on new challenges.

One of the reasons given for not stopping smoking, especially by women, is that they fear that they will gain weight. The weight gain associated with smoking is not just caused by eating more. The body's metabolism changes as a result of eliminating nicotine. One former smoker suggests that we follow her lead. Every time she bemoaned the weight gain, she pictured herself, very thin, dying of lung cancer. It sounds brutal, but it brings the real issues into focus. Remember that if you quit smoking now, your body can recover and within ten years your health risks will be the same as nonsmokers'.

Stress

One reason many of us abuse alcohol or drugs and smoke cigarettes is to try to escape the tremendous stress in our lives. Working parents undergo particular stresses as they face the demands of raising children, busy careers, and trying to find time to spend with their spouses. Each of these endeavors has its own stress factors. Raising children in the modern world is hard. No matter where we live, we have to be concerned with drugs and violence and try to find the right combination of supervision and freedom to both protect our children and teach them to be independent adults. Many of us are in highly competitive jobs. The pressures of keeping up with the information age are huge. What do you do when the boss expects 12 hours a day and you can't/don't want to give it? Finally, it isn't always easy to be married. If you can't find time to put into the relationship, it is going to suffer. None of us wants a marriage to die. We married in order to join forces, but it isn't always easy to keep a relationship thriving in today's stressful world.

We all know how stress feels. The symptoms vary from person to person but they usually include: feeling as though the top of the head is going to blow away (a sign of high blood pressure), racing pulse, breaking out in a sweat, insomnia, a neck that feels as if it's in knots, and intestinal problems such as stomachaches and indigestion. We are also well acquainted with the ways too much stress manifests itself in our behavior. How many times have you found yourself getting very angry at something small, becoming impatient when others aren't moving as quickly as you want them to, always doing (or trying to do) two things at once—such as helping your children with their homework and watching the evening news?

Why do some people seem so much calmer than others? Are they single, childless, and independently wealthy? Of course not (and those people have their own stresses). They have the same demands as the rest of us, their stress load is not so different from ours, but they do react to stress differently from those who always feel as if they are at the end of their rope. It is helpful to realize that we can't eliminate all the factors that cause stress in our lives; rather, we have to work to change the way we react to these situations. Sometimes our reactions to stress actually cause more stress. Can you really help with algebra and listen to the news at the same time, or are you setting yourself up for more stress by having a frustrated teen and a blaring TV in the same room?

Perhaps the most important behavioral aid in controlling our *negative* reactions to stress is to let go of those things over which we have no control. If you are stuck in traffic and going to be late, there is a certain point where you just have to accept the inevitable. If there is a way to get to a telephone, great, but if not, try taking deep breaths instead of pounding your horn. Honking your horn is not going to get you to the meeting any sooner. It will raise your blood pressure, make you sweat, and ruin your mood. Breathing deeply and thinking about what you want to accomplish at the meeting will result in a calm, although tardy, arrival, which certainly makes a better impression than a wild-eyed sweaty executive.

There is little to be gained from losing your temper in no-win situations. We have all witnessed people getting angry at the messenger. Most of us have undoubtedly lost our tempers at the wrong people or reacted much too strongly for the situation. When these temper flares occur, try to calm down. Take the time to figure out what's really bothering you. Anger directed at the individual who can change the situation is much more beneficial than screaming at a person who cannot do a thing to help you. If you feel that your stress level is getting out of control and you can't handle it, consider taking one of the many courses in stress management. Most colleges with adult programs or YMCAs offer these classes. It isn't possible or desirable to eliminate stress entirely from our lives, but it is possible to change the ways we react to it.

It's important to remember that not all reactions to stress are bad. Pressure and stressful situations can motivate us. In extreme situations, we may perform beyond our normal limits, such as in cases of individuals lifting automobiles to save someone trapped beneath. On a smaller scale, many of us know that we react well to crisis. The problems begin if we rely on this surge of energy to get us through all our daily tasks. Again, setting priorities and having realistic expectations can ease the daily load of stress.

Exercise and eating well are excellent aids in controlling how we react to stress. So is laughter. Norman Cousins was convinced he helped prolong his life after the diagnosis of a terminal illness by watching Marx Brothers movies every day. Alcohol and drugs are not real solutions to being uptight. They can make us feel dull and headachy the next day, which slows down our work and shortens our tempers, thereby resulting in more stress. On the other hand, a brisk walk, a good dinner, and private time with our family can help us remember why we are working so hard.

Is Stress Contagious?

The relationship between home and work and how one affects the other seems to be different for men and women. Men tend to judge the "success" of their lives on the way things are going at work—they take the workday home. On the other hand, women tend to take their home to work. The less stress a woman feels at home, the less likely she is to feel stress on the job. It's easy to see how one partner's stress can affect the other. If a man is suffering negative stress with no relief, he will probably have less time, certainly less quality time, for his family. The tension in the home may increase as a result of the man's stress, leading to stress on the wife. In turn, she may take that stress to work and be less productive, causing her male subordinate extra stress, which he will then take home, etc. It's easy to see that the epidemic is passed along from home to office to home. Is there a vaccine against stress?

Unfortunately, the reference to a vaccine is more than a metaphor. It is estimated that stress directly contributes to 50% of all illnesses in the United States. The health-care costs for job-related stress are $200 billion a year. These statistics are influenced by the number of women now in the work force. Women are catching up to men in stress-related illnesses such as heart attacks and ulcers. Researchers are beginning to realize what many people have known instinctively for years—a sound mind makes a healthy body. Studies have proven that the brain has a much greater influence on how our bodies work than was previously suggested. If we are depressed, unhappy, frustrated, or worried, this information is stored and can affect the way our hearts work. It is difficult to do exact studies on emotions, but there is a growing body of evidence that tells us we had better take seriously the relationship between feelings and health.

Doctors have been able to study why some people respond "better" to stress, that is with fewer health problems, than others. They call the ability to handle stress "stress resilience." In a study performed by Raymond Flannery, Jr., assistant professor of psychology at the Harvard Medical School, stress-resilient people were shown to share the following four characteristics:

1. They were committed to a goal and therefore felt that they were pursuing meaningful things.
2. They relaxed at least 15 minutes a day, had regular aerobic exercise, and used a minimum of stimulants.
3. They sought out people and maintained friendships as opposed to being socially isolated.
4. They were not passive about problems. They aggressively sought solutions to problems. In contrast, people who were frequently ill were more likely to do little to change unhappy situations.

None of these positive practices is beyond any of us. Rather, the stress-resilient men and women seemed to incorporate many of the points we have been discussing. They have control in their lives. They have identified and maintained goals. They get a moderate amount of exercise and enjoy the company of other people. It sounds easy, but many of us have gotten away from these common-sense ways of life. How can we change what went wrong?

Changing Inner Stereotypes

As we learn that the way we feel about ourselves influences the way our body works, it makes sense to take some time to examine our feelings about ourselves. An interesting psychological experiment has adults look at a particular picture and then asks them to make up a story about the picture. The picture consists of two adults and a child. The overwhelming majority of people who participate in this experiment tell a story from the point of view of the child. They might begin by saying "The child is wondering, the child is thinking, the child wants, etc." Regardless of the age of the participant, most people identify with the child.

How many of us are leading adult lives with the same thoughts about ourselves that we were given as children? We say "given" because most of us develop our sense of self-esteem through our parents. Our parents are role models for behavior as well as teachers of how we look at ourselves. If our parents concentrated on telling us we were capable of anything we wanted to do, we probably grew up eager to try new experiences and had confidence that we could learn new things. We weren't demoralized by failure because we knew that we could try again. On the other hand, many of us were taught fear as children—fear of failure, fear of disappointment, fear of ridicule. Sadly, parents often teach fear out of love. They love their children and don't want them to be hurt. As a result, they often shelter their children or fail to encourage them to take risks. The good news is that you are an adult now and can listen to the way you think about yourself and correct those messages that you do not like.

Mental messages are internal role models. They are just as important as physical role models in determining many of our daily decisions. Many of us have had to deal with the gender models assigned at birth. We have been successful at overcoming the gender limitations. For example, many men were brought up thinking that emotions were inappropriate responses to events. Rather than allowing an emotion to surface, they were taught by example that they should keep emotions in check, concentrating on reason instead. Men are now learning that they not only can care for their children, but they can be very good caretakers. This entry into a new area is part of risk taking. The same is true for women. Learning to negotiate a deal, making big financial decisions, and working outside the home have been new territories that many women have dared to try, explore, and conquer.

The same energy applied to breaking external stereotypes can also be applied to our inner typecasting. The bookworm can make speeches, the entertainer can have a serious job, the strong silent types can learn to express their feelings, and mommy's little helper can spend time alone writing a book. We all know the inner roles we were assigned, but few of us have taken the time to listen to them recently. We do not realize to what extent old messages may be holding us back. We identify with the child in the psychology experiment because we still think of ourselves in terms assigned at childhood.

As we free up the inner rules, we are able to do the things needed to become stress resilient. We see that we are talented and capable of going after something new. We recognize that we are likable and begin to reach out for new friends as well as devote some time to maintaining or re-establishing old friendships. We understand that our lives are important and begin to work toward making them healthier. We accept that we can change the way we feel about ourselves and do not accept passively someone else's assessment of our worth.

Things to Remember About Health Problems

- Depression can affect anyone.
- Teach yourself to think optimistically.
- Women, don't ruminate!
- If the dependency quiz helps you identify a problem, don't ignore it. Problems do not disappear on their own.
- Get to know your inner self. Make sure your internal messages are up-to-date and positive.

13

Relaxation, or the Lost Art of Contemplation

During the fast-paced and workaholic decade of the '80s, many of us forgot to relax. Much of the '80s was about competition: how much, how fast, and how to. If we weren't busy working, we were busy trying to do all the things we thought had to get done. Too often, the closest we came to relaxing was dropping exhausted in front of a TV set, too tired to do anything but focus our eyes on what we were told was entertainment. We felt as though there was no time for sitting around and watching the world go by. Instead, it seemed that our awareness of life was accompanied by and filtered through the sound bites of the evening news.

Our to-do lists grew with every article we read or with each news show we watched. Many of us lived through the last ten years feeling that we were always working and always tired. Maybe it wasn't a matter of forgetting to relax as much as it was a sense that there was no time to relax. Rather than thinking of relaxation as a necessary commodity, we thought of it as a reward. Relaxing came after the day's work was done. The problem was (and is) that there was always more work, at home as well as at the office. How could we take a break, for an hour, a day, two weeks, when we still had so much work to do?

Is there a way out of this condition? Is the expression "stop and smell the roses" old-fashioned and out-of-date? How do we find a balance between requirements and rest? How do we slow down or cut down so that we can really enjoy and savor the full lives we live? Can we shift our priorities to include invisible accomplishments?

Competitor Versus Couch Potato

During the last decade, many of the things that added to the richness of life, such as friendship and feeling part of a community, seemed to lose value under the constant barrage of how to improve oneself. Jane Fonda urged us to feel the burn, jogging led to running, running to marathons, and marathons to triathlons. The tremendous competitive pressure stopped many of us before we got started.

On the other hand, many of us relished the opportunity to compete. Women, especially, enjoyed the chance to explore and show off their physical and mental abilities. Earning money challenged us in ways vacuuming never did. There was always something more for us to try. In many ways, the information age was a boon and a blessing. Men and women both were exposed to new ideas and examples. As we read about a 50-year-old running in his or her first marathon, we became inspired to emulate. The problem is that after hearing about the older first-time marathoner, we heard about the whiz kids of law and medicine. We were bombarded by stories of people who did it all. Rather than inspired, we became discouraged by our own sense that all this excelling was beyond us. Some of us didn't try to do it all, and we were labeled for it. Those of us who admitted that we liked to sit around and do nothing were called "couch potatoes." The battle lines were drawn between two very extreme groups. Few of us want to sit around all day and switch TV stations any more than we want to train for four hours a day to have the pleasure of a long, grueling ocean swim followed by an exhausting bicycle race, topped off by a marathon. Surely, there is a life-style that strikes a balance between these two extremes. The superathletes work and compete for relaxation; the so-called couch potatoes live their lives outside the office through television. Most of us fall somewhere between these groups.

What happened to relaxation? Did we lose it, forget it, or throw it away? For many of us, the answer is a little bit of all three. We lost it because we didn't have time to relax. Whatever time had once been devoted to leisure was eaten away by longer hours at a competitive workplace, longer commutes as traffic increased, and more tasks to be done once we did get home. It's easy to see why many of us opt for alcohol and TV when we do have a moment. To some extent, both dull us to our daily demands.

Another factor in losing relaxation is perhaps a lost sense that relaxation is vital to our mental and physical well-being. During the '80s, it seemed as though we were weak if we wanted to do nothing. Machines worked for us around the clock, many factories began having night shifts, and corporate law firms and investment companies began to employ people throughout the wee small hours. Department stores and malls began to remain open late nearly every night. As financial responsibilities increased, it became harder and harder for a person to say no to more work. Stressed out from so much work, it became harder to say no to spending the money we worked so hard to earn, which led to debt, which led to more work, and so on.

Reclaiming the Weekend

Weekends used to be times for letting our minds unwind from the workweek. We spent time with our families and friends. In the '80s, with more of us working outside the home, weekends were frequently taken up with laundry, cleaning, and even catching up on work we didn't get done during the week. This behavior was to some extent necessary. With more people having jobs outside the home, the full-time homemaker role traditionally filled by women was largely abandoned. Many people failed to value this work in the first place. Few of us really thought about the hard work it takes to keep a home and family running smoothly and happily. As women went to work outside the home, no plan was put in place by society to pick up the slack. Because the work was devalued to start with, few seemed to think that it would be difficult to fit in, in their spare time. Obviously this "spare-time" concept was not the way most women looked at the work they had to do at home, but if they wanted to pursue a career outside homemaking or if they needed the money to meet their families' financial needs, housework had to be fitted in around and after "real work."

Now that we know that housework is important, the key is finding out when to do it. We also need to rethink whose responsibility it is to get the chores done so that we can all find time to relax. Try some of the following ideas to get your weekends back:

1. Make a list of every chore that must be done every week. Be as specific as possible, i.e., how many loads of laundry, how many rooms to be vacuumed, etc.

2. Inventory your workers. That is, realistically figure out what your spouse and children can do. Five-year-olds might have a hard time with mops, but they are great at stripping beds and dusting.

3. Have a family discussion regarding each job and assign weekly tasks. If possible, let each person have a say in his or her assignments. We all do better at those things we choose ourselves.

4. Set aside a family time for getting the jobs done. If everyone is working at the same time, morale is high and it's harder to avoid a task. Your time could be Wednesday evening or Saturday morning—whatever you choose. It is best, though, to avoid Sunday night. Last-minute scurrying starts the week on a jangled note.

5. Don't think of the weekend as a time to catch up on office work. Often, by thinking that we can do something later, we are really just putting it off. If there was no later, we'd be more likely to work more efficiently. Make a vow to quit catching up on weekday responsibilities on the weekend.

6. Have at least one pleasure goal per weekend. It can be starting a new novel, watching a sports event, taking a two-

hour nap. Give this goal the same weight that you would any other. Discuss it with your spouse—ask for his help in holding you to it.

Once you've devised a plan for mundane, time-consuming, but important housework, it's time to think about relaxing. Most of us know we're overburdened, and we may be beginning to know why —too much to do and not enough time to do it—but we don't necessarily know the way out of this situation. Some of the answers we try to help you find throughout the book are specific: make goals and talk about them with your partner, learn to say no, organize yourself at work to get the maximum out of your time, and learn to delegate.

The Puritan Work Ethic

Before we can reclaim relaxation, it is important that we value it. For many of us, it is difficult to do something purely for pleasure. We have constant messages to ourselves and others about the way we spend our time. Do you ever call yourself words like "bad" or "lazy" when you read a book instead of doing the laundry? Do you feel that you deserve praise only when you are doing something visibly productive? Many of us were raised with this idea, and to a great extent it is a natural inheritance from our forefathers.

Other than those born to Native American culture, all of us are the descendants of immigrants. Many left their country of birth in order to find freedom, both political and economic. Our family histories are full of stories about working up from nothing, the long walks to school through the snow, and the constant sacrifice necessary to gain a piece of the dream for their children and grandchildren. Many of these stories are true, but our ancestors had fun too. Don't forget the stories of the clambakes and the picnics and the trips to visit Aunt Ida in the next town. Remember, too, that many of our ancestors were raised in homes where a day of the week was set aside for religion. With all the hard work, it was understood that a day without work was important.

It's important to know how and what we define as productive. It seems hard to believe, but many of us need help in learning how to relax. Perhaps more accurately, we need help in loosening our goals regarding leisure time. If that's hard, you might want to try a few of the following tips.

1. Keep work and play separate. Get away from the office. If you enjoy playing tennis with a colleague, great, but as you talk afterwards, try to stay away from office politics or events. Ask your teammate what he/she thinks about some current news item, a new movie, or the latest public scandal. Don't be afraid to laugh. If you worry about revealing your personal thoughts to a colleague, find a new tennis partner.

2. Don't procrastinate on fun. Have you always said you would learn to sail, play golf, develop and print your own photographs, or cook with a wok—as soon as you had time? Well, the time is now. If you haven't studied a recent bulletin from your YMCA or local college, you may be surprised at the wide array of continuing education. Learning something is a wonderful way to remind ourselves that our minds still work. It builds our egos and improves our sense of ourselves.

3. Try to keep competition to a minimum during your leisure activities—unless you're an individual who relaxes through competition. If playing bridge is as much a social occasion as an intellectual one for you, be sure to play bridge with people who like to talk and play at the same time. Leisure time is fun. If you feel you must put up a facade at play, then you will derive little pleasure or benefit from your time off.

4. Do what you want to do with your leisure time, not what you think you should do. We know this time is precious, so be sure to enjoy it. At the same time, don't be afraid to try something new. If you and your spouse want to find something that you can enjoy together, it might be fun to try something new each month until you hit on an activity that pleases both of you.

5. Don't feel guilty about having fun! If you really can't escape the need to justify your free-time activities, try saying to yourself that it will make you a better spouse, parent, and individual if you learn to recharge by relaxing.

Making a Commitment
to Relaxation

We've talked about establishing goals at work and in the family. It's important to know what you want out of fun, too. Do you want to learn a sport? Many of us, especially women, were not encouraged to learn sports as we were growing up. It isn't too late. Many people take up tennis in their 40s and 50s. Would you like to take an art class? Many find a studio art class—pottery, silk screening, painting, weaving, etc.—a wonderful way to relax after the office. You probably are using different mind functions from those you use at work. Instead of analyzing or using your critical thinking abilities, you are working to express another side of yourself, a different, more obviously creative side than usually called upon in our jobs.

It doesn't matter what you choose. What is important is to choose something that you really want to do. You can choose something as a family or something on your own. Don't be afraid to want to try something new. If people laugh at you, ignore them—they are jealous. Remember that you are working on getting rid of what you "ought" to be doing and concentrating on what you truly want to do. After you make a choice, make a commitment to stick with it. We've all got a closet somewhere with uncompleted projects such as birdhouses or sweaters. Those past projects can haunt us now as we try to change our daily lives. Forget the past (you might want to clean out that closet) and decide that you are committed to the first stage of this new personal and relaxing activity. Now it's a goal that is as important as the other goals on your master list. As is the case with all goals, it's now important to figure out the interim steps needed to obtain your goal.

For example, if you've always wanted to learn to play tennis, you first need to know what lessons and courts are available in your area. You might begin by looking in the yellow pages under "recreation" or by calling the United States Lawn Tennis Association. By doing a little investigation by phone, you can see what your options are. Many public parks and recreation centers have lessons for beginners. Talk to friends who play tennis and ask them about the facilities in your area. You might even be able to borrow a racket and avoid spending money until you know what you want and need. You might want to undertake this adventure with a friend, but don't be afraid to do something on your own. Chances are you will meet other beginners who could become practice and playing partners. Don't forget to give yourself a reward as you accomplish your goals. As you improve, you might think of buying a tennis outfit or a racket, or subscribing to a tennis magazine.

It's been said that college is wasted on the young. Going back to school is something that has enriched many adults. The actual process of learning something new or exploring in depth a particular interest is a wonderful way to relax. For many of us, school was a burden in our youth. We were unable to appreciate the luxury of learning. You might be surprised how much you enjoy going back to school now that it is a choice rather than a necessity.

Almost every community offers evening and weekend classes. Call and order the catalogs. You will see that there are courses in many fields, from cooking and languages to computers and literature. In addition to the variety of courses, there are many options regarding the length of the class. There are one-day seminars and 12-week courses of study. It's possible to take classes for credit if you want to work toward a degree. Another choice is to take a class for no credit. This might be a good idea if you know that you want the class to help motivate you, but don't want to put yourself in a competitive grade situation. Taking a class for no credit could be a way to remind yourself that you're attending this class for pleasure. Also, if you're taking a class for pleasure, try to avoid work-related subjects. Don't cross the work and pleasure lines. If you are in school for professional improvement, you might want to try the nonschool route for relaxation.

A word to single people: classes, athletic or academic, are one of the best ways to meet people. Shared interests are a given, as you already know that you share the interest of the class. The class offers an easy nonpressured place to meet, and it's a great help in starting a conversation. Groups that form in classes can help set up a structure that will continue after the class is over. If you met in a class studying short stories, you can continue to meet and discuss stories that the group selects.

For those of you who are married, it's important to discuss your need for outside activities with your spouse. As we said earlier, you and your partner may well decide that you would like to undertake a new hobby together. Besides providing motivation for one another, it's a great way to find more time to be together. You may also decide that you each have different interests that can't be combined. That's fine. Discuss your individual desires and see if you can work out a plan that provides support and encouragement for each person.

Your children also can be helpers in your decision to try something new. If they play ice hockey, you might take up ice skating during their practice time. Many families enjoy a day of riding bicycles. It doesn't matter what you do, but playing together as a family is a wonderful way to find time to spend together. Take pleasure and pride in each other's accomplishments.

Relaxation—Learn to Give It Value

If there is one point to make in this chapter, it's that taking a break is just as worthy of your time and effort as work. We've learned that relaxation is a learned skill that is as valuable as delegation or time management. In fact, delegation and time management are the keys to relaxation. We must regard time to get away from it all with the same seriousness that we regard the rest of our lives. When we recharge, we give value to that which requires recharging.

Don't fall into the trap of thinking you are weak or frivolous by wondering what it is all about or because you want more out of life. Remember that you are working in order to have certain things. The key is to know what the things are. Try to avoid the treadmill of working to exist. Do feel that you can want intangible things in your life. There is nothing wrong with having fun or wanting to work at something others may not understand.

Don't ignore your own needs to take a break. You may find that taking a moment to smell the roses helps you see your world more clearly.

Things to Remember
About Relaxation

- Relaxation is vital to your mental and physical well-being.
- Reclaim your weekend!
- Keep work and play separate. Try to keep competition to a minimum during leisure activities.
- Establish goals for fun. It's important to know what you want out of your valuable time.

14

Finding the Time to Relax

Many of us laugh at the idea of developing a hobby, taking a class, or reading a book. We laugh because there is no time for *one more* thing in our lives. Those of us who are married think that it might be easier if we were single, that there would be one less schedule to factor in. At the same time, those of us who are single think that a partner would be an answer to child care, enabling us to get out on our own one night a week. It's rough on everyone, single or married. The question is the same: How do you find time to do what you *want* to do? As we said earlier, the biggest obstacle to your goal is finding the time in which to relax.

Less Television, More Time

The time pressures are real, but there is a simple, although some-what radical, approach that you might want to try: quit watching television. Or at least, watch less television. Before dismissing this idea as foolish, try keeping a television journal. Put a notebook on top of the television (or on top of each television if you are a multi-TV house), and write down when you turn it on and when you turn it off. After a week of jotting down times, add up the hours.

This is not an exercise to make a value judgment or to induce guilt. It's a way of trying to help you find time to do things that you do not have time to do. A good exercise plan can take as little as three hours a week (30 minutes walking, five times a week, plus the time spent getting to and from your walking path); most classes do not exceed four hours per week; you can learn tennis in an hour lesson three times a week. The list goes on. You get the point. The average person spends 30 hours a week watching television. Can you give up an hour a day of television? We're not suggesting unplugging completely, although that might be an interesting experiment, but rather that you analyze the amount of time you spend in front of the TV.

How many of us say, "Oh, I don't really watch that much television. Half the time it's on, I'm barely watching." If you turn it off, you might find that you were watching more than you thought. You might find that without the constant drone of television you are wandering around, not sure what to do without the ever-present pull on your time and attention. Television acts as a tether from which we are reluctant to stray. Our movements are limited to actions that can be performed in ever-ready eye range of the screen. When we aren't sitting and staring, our ears are listening, telling us to swivel our eyes to the screen for some juicy action, or reminding us that the ad break is over.

Whatever the rationalizations, television has taken over our leisure time more than any other modern invention. We are not free to move at our own pace. We are in step with the carefully planned network schedules. Children may be most at risk by watching constant television. With television as a main activity, children are not developing their own minds and imaginations. Remember the silly games you would invent to occupy an afternoon? Our children are losing this skill.

It is often said that necessity is the mother of invention; we don't think of solutions to problems unless we need to. As our children sit and watch, usually joined by parents, we need to realize that we are all losing the ability to entertain ourselves as well as losing the time in which to do it. How can we expect our children to be self-reliant and inventive if they spend most of their time outside school being force-fed entertainment?

Getting Away from It All

Vacations offer us a chance to change our daily habits. Besides helping break the TV habit, vacations allow us a chance to change our priorities and to regain our perspective about what's really important in our lives. The clock becomes an ally instead of an enemy. Depending upon the type of vacation you plan—active or nonactive or a combination of the two—you can rediscover the joys of bounding out of bed early or sleeping until noon. It's easier to get out of bed when an adventure calls, whether it's Epcot or an empty beach. It's easier to wake up when the thought of a nap later in the day isn't heresy. It's also easier to turn over and go back to sleep when there is no pressure of car pools or early-morning meetings.

Different families choose different kinds of vacations. The same family chooses differently from year to year depending upon children's ages, finances, and time available. Some of us grew up in families where the two-week vacation in summer was a ritual. For others, vacations were not the norm. For those of us from farming families or whose parents owned small businesses, family vacations were rare, if not impossible.

Different families also make various decisions regarding whether they want to plan an outing for the whole family, or a week where the parents can remember that they are a couple. Again, depending upon your time and financial leeway, you may try to do both during the year. Perhaps you and your spouse can get away for a week or at least one long weekend during the year. It's a great way to renew and bring freshness to a marriage. Regarding children and vacations, it's important to remember that there are no rules. You are not a bad parent if you don't want to spend every minute of your spare time with your children.

Some Advantages of Traveling with Children

1. You won't have to arrange for baby-sitters and, therefore, will probably worry less.

2. You will get to know your kids in new ways as they are exposed to new surroundings. They will notice things you might have missed.

3. You can learn something with your children and thereby break down some stereotypes about learning and growing. It's good for kids to see that they are just as capable of learning history as their parents. It's also a great example for your children to see that adults don't know everything and actually enjoy learning new things.

Some Disadvantages of Traveling with Children

1. Fancy restaurants and exotic food are probably not possible with children under 12. Romance will also have to take a back seat on family vacations.

2. Long days of sight-seeing are hard on kids under eight or nine. Sleeping in unfamiliar beds also can be difficult for youngsters. It's usually a good idea to take along your child's pillow or favorite stuffed animal to ease anxieties.

3. Teenagers usually like to be as far from parents as possible. Don't let memories or fantasies cloud your judgment on the reality of teenage behavior.

Whatever you decide, it's best to be realistic that the vacations will be different, depending upon whether you travel with or without the kids. Where you go and what you do should take into account whether the younger set will have fun. The ages of your children and the success with which they interact should also have a bearing on your destination. If there is an older child who can help with a younger one, great. On the other hand, there are times when it is best not to count on siblings getting along. Be realistic. Don't expect cooperation on the road if you do not have it at home. Once again, it isn't easy to predict teenage behavior. If you are planning on their cooperation, make sure you discuss individual responsibilities beforehand.

If You Take the Kids

Traveling with children is perhaps the ultimate proof of Murphy's Law. If something can go wrong, it will. How many of us have cleaned up after a retching child by the side of a road or temporarily lost a child in an unfamiliar shopping mall? We've all seen the too-bright eyes of a feverish child as we're heading for the Magic Kingdom. On the other hand, we all know it's the kids who have often saved us from huge vacation glitches. They are the ones who say things like "Dad, is that suitcase supposed to be hanging down from the luggage rack?" or "That sign said no more gas for fifty miles, how far can we drive on empty?" Children are also the ones who grab your hand on the beach late at night, asking how far the ocean goes and what's on the other side. Their amazement at seeing something new, whether in nature or man-made, often erases much parental tension created by the trip itself.

A successful vacation is helped by careful planning. When you go on vacation with your children it's important to remember that diversion helps. Children's attention spans are shorter than ours, and rarely do youngsters relish trips in a car or plane or train. Beautiful scenery is usually completed wasted on them. We might wish they would sleep during transportation to and from our destinations, but we know it's rare. Whether traveling by car, train, or plane, here are a few tips to help your children have fun during travel:

1. Have a bag of gift-wrapped small toys or treats to hand out during the trip. Depending on the age of your children, these might be comic books, hand games on the order of Rubik's Cube, or a small stack of construction paper and crayons.
2. Fresh fruit, individual boxes of juice, and peanut-butter crackers are good car snacks. Candy bars and soft drinks can result in a sugar "high," making overactivity a real problem.
3. Cassette players with earphones enable children to listen to their own music (and keep them from distracting the driver or other passengers). Books on tape are another good idea. A story geared to your child's interests helps pass the time as well as expose your child to the fun of a good story.

4. If you are traveling by car, try to give each child a specific responsibility. One might be in charge of the drink cooler, another of keeping track of your progress on a map. Most children are not familiar with geography. A road atlas can be a great way to teach them how to read a map.

5. Other good teaching and entertainment tools are brochures and books dealing with your destination. Get your children involved in learning where they are going. Don't forget to listen to their ideas regarding the daily agenda. The more participation they have in planning the activities, the more involved they'll become. Vacations are a great time to get to know your kids outside the usual family roles.

6. If you are traveling by plane, be sure to remember some specific snacks to help relieve air pressure's effect on the ears. Chewing gum and hard candy are good for older kids; bottles or safety cups of juice are good for the younger set.

It's worth an hour or two of planning for the travel part of your vacation in order to assure a smooth trip. Everyone is happier and tension levels are lower when the kids have fun too. A positive attitude and good humor on the adults' part will certainly help your kids get into the spirit of the trip. If some things go wrong and you all lose your temper, it's OK. What will remain is the memory of the fun you had.

Vacations—Extended Family Pros and Cons

Another factor in vacation planning is whether to include a visit with extended family members. We all know that many families are physically farther apart now than ever before. Career opportunities, lifestyle choices, love and marriage are all reasons for moving away from our home town. Most of us have parents and siblings in other cities. The ramifications of this extended family structure are many. Nowhere is this dynamic more powerful and influential than in planning vacations.

The two main times we have to visit with our extended families are during holidays and family vacations. Visiting with family members without the daily pressure of the office offers us a chance to catch up and stay in touch with those we love. It's fun to watch our children get to know their cousins and aunts, uncles and grandparents. Another advantage is that family vacations are frequently cheaper than solo family trips. Staying with relatives saves on the expense of hotel rooms and restaurant meals.

The downside of visiting relatives for a vacation is the potential for arguments and stress arising from some of the same factors that make visiting relatives a good idea. Other adults may discipline children in ways that contradict our personal views. Staying with relatives makes for close quarters and usually makes it impossible for families to have any privacy. And even the most well-adjusted of us can have a tough time when thrown back into our family of origin. Old labels such as "the smart one," "the fun one," or "the serious one" can rekindle old arguments. Even worse, sometimes we may fall into the old behavior that caused the label in the first place.

If you do plan on spending part of your vacation with relatives, here are a few pointers to make the trip more pleasurable:

1. If you are the visitor, treat the host family with the same good manners that you would use when visiting a friend. Arrive with gifts, which can be as simple or as elaborate as your budget allows. Food is always good. Say "thank you" frequently, and remember that you are the guest.

2. Be neat! Keep your clothes off the floor and patrol your children's belongings. In the kitchen, make sure that your family does more than their share of the dishes.

3. If you are the host family, *do* ask for help. Do not suffer in silence! Men, make sure your wife doesn't carry the burden of your family.

4. *Do not* bring up old arguments. These visits are supposed to be pleasurable. Trying to "win" or resolve an ancient rivalry is self-defeating. If you have a grudge that needs to be aired, don't do it while on vacation. Plan a separate, private time and make your agenda known.

5. As with all vacations, advance planning will help guarantee

a good trip. As a guest, make sure you arrive and depart when you say you will. As a host, have some outings planned. Sitting around waiting for someone to suggest an activity is frustrating, especially for children. Even if you and your sister want to sit around and chat, remember to have some sort of planned activity for the kids.

Another option for a family vacation is to plan an extended family get-together at a neutral spot. This can help with territorial arguments and provide an opportunity for privacy within a large group. You and your partner will have an easier time getting away for a private dinner if you are not staying with parents or siblings. Resort expenses can be shared. Older and younger children can be grouped together for the best age-specific activity.

Unfortunately, many of us have the problem of *not* wanting to spend our valuable time off with members of our extended families. At least we don't want to spend all our vacation time with them. Or we don't want to spend time off with our spouse's family. How many of us have said to friends "It's easy to be with my folks, but John's/Mary's family is completely different." For others, being with in-laws is actually easier than being with one's own family since past history and the pain of separation are missing. Whatever the case, there is no more important place for spouses to be completely honest with one another than in their need to join or avoid other family members during vacation.

Too often, we feel that we get roped into spending much of our valued off-time with our extended families, often losing out on private time with our spouses and children. In order to be "good" children or "close" siblings, we ignore our need for time to explore personal desires and relationships outside the birth family. The concerns are real. No one lives forever. There is no more delicate balance to try to achieve than being a part of an extended family.

The problem, of course, is that once again we are pulled in many directions. Some of the pull comes from those in our families who love us and want more than a Sunday phone call. More of the pull we put on ourselves as we try to make those we love happy. And of course, another pull is *wanting* to spend time with those we love.

A source of stress is being close to someone and at the same time being unable to see them more than once or twice a year. Add the complexities of your spouse's extended family and it is easy to see why vacations, where to go and whom to go with, are a potential source of tension.

Perhaps a key to deciding when to use vacation time for a trip to visit relatives is to be honest about how much it means to you. The first factor should be to gauge the amount of fun you will have on the proposed trip. By fun, we mean whether the trip will relax you. If spending time with the family you grew up with is always a source of pleasure and fun, you're both lucky and unusual.

After figuring the fun factor, think about how you will feel if you miss out on an annual visit with a sibling or parent. A possible solution might be to plan on a weekend trip to visit without involving your spouse or children. Most of us have at least some tension present during family visits. We add stress to our lives by trying to be spouse, parent, child, and sibling at the same time.

Perhaps the best way to guarantee private vacation time for your family is, once again, to plan it first. It's hard for siblings and parents to argue against nonrefundable deposits. In the same vein, after you and your spouse have the "what do you really want to do" discussion, let your family know what time you expect to spend with them. For example, "we'll miss you at the beach, but we'll see you for Thanksgiving." Once decisions are made, it's easier to field family requests. The key is *making* the decision as opposed to either deciding by default or promising to visit but never having it happen.

You Don't Have to Be Married to Have This Problem

Family visits are not just a problem for married couples. Single adults often find that their families expect them to spend all holidays and vacations with them. Even if the single adult is a parent, family members can easily expect that you can be the one to travel. Singles, too, should decide ahead of time which time is sacred to them.

Two single friends figured out how to handle their families' expectations by joining forces. They were both pressured to "come home" for Thanksgiving and Christmas. Both found the two trips within weeks of each other difficult, expensive, and tiring. Both have full-time jobs and many friends, and happen to be excellent cooks. In their mid-30s, they were more than ready to have at least one holiday celebration in their own homes. They made their own tradition by inviting friends together to share Thanksgiving. They explained to their families that they were now hosting Thanksgiving dinner together. They continued to travel for the Christmas holidays, but were able to counter their families' pleas by explaining that they had full plans for the holiday time. Their seeming defection was softened by the promise of an immediate Christmas visit.

On the other hand, vacation time can be a great time for singles to join in a family outing. If one of your siblings is single, think of asking if she would like to be included in a big vacation. It's hard for a single person to take a cross-country trip alone or go to Disney World solo. An aunt or uncle can be a real advantage to a traveling family. Kids tend to behave a little better with a less-familiar adult around. Aunts and uncles can often get through to older kids when parents, by the very nature of being parents, are ineffective. Finally, parents can often get a break from the daily responsibility of children by ceding a few hours of responsibility to these other adults.

Whatever you choose to do for vacation, remember to keep your expectations realistic. Not every trip is an unqualified success. If things go wrong, try to keep your sense of humor. Learn from mistakes and plan differently next time. Families need different things at different times.

Things to Remember About Finding the Time to Relax

- Cutting down on TV time can help you find time for individual and family pursuits.
- On vacation, plan entertainment for your kids to have while traveling.
- Involve children in vacation choices and activities.
- Don't let extended family take over all your vacation time—unless that's what works for you.

15

How Volunteer Service Can Help Balance Your Life

Throughout this book we have discussed the relationship between balance and establishing priorities. How do we learn to know what are realistic self-expectations? When is it OK to say "enough"? It is important to know what matters to you and then to make time for those things. Without balance, we often miss out on the very things that mean the most to us. We are always busy, but we too often feel empty.

Many people have found that the solution to this dilemma is volunteer work. Through working with people and groups that need her talents, an individual is able to find meaning in the way she conducts her life. For some, working for something other than money is a way to achieve inner happiness and fulfillment. As they become involved in issues and people that matter to them and their communities, their lives seem less fractured and begin to take on a higher importance. The connections between people seem closer and the concept of "fellow man" becomes less abstract.

It may seem strange to talk about volunteer work—adding another responsibility to already busy lives—but, in fact, for many this commitment has helped them find balance in their lives. Karen Lindauer was employed at CBS when she began working with boarder babies (infants of drug-addicted mothers or others who are unable to care for their newborn babies) at a hospital in New York City.

> . . . there was something lacking in me, in my job, and being able to release all the stuff, all the love, and all the feelings, it was just like glue. It just worked, it was the right thing for me to do. I was also looking for a career change at the time, and since then, I don't need a career change, I really don't. Because it fulfills everything. . . . What's nice for me is that I am becoming a woman I really admire, and just the job can't do that.

Another aspect of doing volunteer or service work is that it is a chance for us to work at what we truly love, not just something that pays enough to live on. (Ideally, our job should be work we truly love, but this is not always possible.) This sharing of ourselves can and should be from our hearts, not our heads. It is a time when we can be free to choose exactly what we want to do. It is a time to think about reaching into our inner dreams and fulfilling them while helping others. If you have always wanted to teach or if you love to cook or if you know you could play the piano as long as someone would listen, here's your chance. There are schools, church kitchens, and senior citizens programs eager for your talent. If you never have time to read a book, find a group that reads to the visually impaired.

Volunteer work need not take advantage of the same skills that earn your living. For example, lawyers shouldn't think that the only "valuable" skills they might have to offer are their legal skills. For many of us, service work offers the chance to use skills that do not have another outlet. As you read this chapter, keep an open mind to the kinds of things you might want to investigate. Be creative; don't limit your opportunities.

How Do I Get Started?

Some of us may know exactly what kind of volunteer work we want to do. There may be a cause or group whose work we admire and want to be part of. Congratulations! Call them. For most of us, the decision is a bit more complex because we really do not know what we want to do. Also, there is a problem in separating what we know we could do and what we would like to do. You may be a great typist or a whiz with numbers, but really want to pursue volunteer work that doesn't use these skills. That's great. Don't limit your horizons.

It's important to take some time to decide how and where you want to give your time. The happier you are at the work, the more you will be able to give. Volunteer work need not be a sacrifice. Ideally, it can be a joy. Tapping your own resources and sharing them with others is a wonderful way to learn about yourself as well as give something to others. Think about the following questions as you work to discover where you would like to expand your life.

1. *Why do you want to do volunteer work?* For example, if you want to feel part of a team and more connected with people in your community, look for opportunities that provide this benefit. Don't take on a task that might be isolating. It is important to talk honestly both with yourself and with any potential organizations about what you want and what you know you can give.

2. *What are your energy patterns?* Do you wake up early on Saturday morning eager to start your day or do you like to enjoy sleeping a little later when you have the chance? There is no right or wrong way to be. Different people have different energy patterns. Are you exhausted at the end of a typical workday or do you find that there is energy to spare? Take advantage of these patterns as you try to find the best times to work. Don't use volunteer work as a way to find self-discipline you feel is lacking. For example, don't volunteer for an 8 A.M. job in order to make yourself get up. Chances are, you'll resent the work and/or be late.

3. *Do you like to create ideas or implement them?* For example, if you know that you do not want any more major responsibilities in your life, do not volunteer to be a committee head. Make sure that you are happy with your level of responsibility. This is a great opportunity to let someone else take the bigger burden.

4. *How do you best relate to people?* Do you like groups or one-on-one interactions? Do you thrive on a little confusion or are you at your best when you have time to think and respond? Once more, the better you know yourself and your specific skills, the easier it will be for you to work at your maximum efficiency.

5. *What do you need to feel appreciated?* Do you like to see your name in print, hear applause, or do you prefer more private approval? It isn't important what you like, but it is important that you be honest about it.

6. *What kind of environment is best for you?* Do hospitals depress you? Do children drive you crazy? Are you happiest when you are physically active? Work with your strengths in choosing the best environment for you.

7. *Do you have any personal negatives?* If you hate the telephone and really are not very good talking to strangers, it is best that you not end up a phone volunteer. Be realistic.

Some of these questions may be more important to you than others. The main point is to give some time to choosing your volunteer work. Don't sign the first list that comes around. Many people are motivated as a result of a tragedy such as the death of a friend or family member, and often they can provide wonderful service to others in similar situations. At the same time, it is important to make sure that this is the best group for you at this time. Once again, be sure to discuss any personal motivations with the placement coordinator.

How Much Time Do I Have to Give?

You are going to need to think about how much time you have to give to this endeavor. The best advice is to start small. You can always increase your hours. No one needs a volunteer who is unable to keep a commitment. Realistically, look at the hours you have to give. Do you have a day a year, a day a month, a few hours each week? What are the effects on your family if you take this time for others? If you currently feel pressed for time to spend with your children and spouse, make sure that your volunteer work won't add to those feelings.

There is a group that needs you no matter how little time you think you have to offer. For example, many organizations have instituted "walk-a-thons." These walks are ways to earn money for a group as well as ways to publicize each group's particular cause. In addition, a once-a-year walk requires a small amount of time and is an activity that can involve the whole family.

It is best to have an idea of the hours you can give *before* getting involved with a group. Don't let yourself be swept up in early enthusiasm. Be sure to stick to your own ideas of what you can do. It is important to evaluate this new activity over a period of time. Start slowly and give yourself a chance to become comfortable. As you work with a group you will have a chance to see how it operates and know more clearly how you best fit together.

Evaluating Your Skills and Talents

If you are like most people, you may not have a grasp of all the things that you do well. Pay attention to the things you do each day and transfer those tasks into skills and abilities. By skills we mean specific areas in which you have some training. This could be as varied as computer expertise or auto mechanics. You need not be an expert to consider something a skill, but you should have enough expertise to know what you can and cannot do. Are your computer skills in word processing, spreadsheets, desktop publishing, or all three? Are you a licensed auto mechanic or an expert on cars manufactured before 1965?

In addition to specific skills, you probably know areas in which you are talented. Think of the things you *know* you can do. Some people are very good at asking for money; others know that they possess the ability to lead a group. Some have a gift with children; others can sell. Whatever it is that you enjoy doing because you are good at it is something of great value to an organization. Make a list of these talents and refer to them when you talk with potential organizations.

Finding the Right
Organization for You

Now that you've got an idea of why you want to do volunteer work, what you want to do, and what you have to offer in terms of time and skills, it's time to look for the right group. Most organizations' budgets have been cut. In contrast to the paid job market, the volunteer job market is wide open. It is hard to imagine that there is not a group suitable for everyone. It will probably be harder for you to decide which group to work with than to find a group that wants you.

As with most endeavors, the best place to begin is usually with family and friends. Talk to people about their experiences with various organizations. Often a person will learn about a group through someone who has benefited from their services. Another way to find people who need your time and talents is to look through your mail at the many groups that solicit donations. If you've begun to know what you want, you will begin to see many ways to fulfill your desires just by paying attention to the people around you.

Don't just think in terms of large organizations. There are many smaller groups that might benefit from your expertise. You might take some time to research opportunities close to home. In addition to working within your own neighborhood, you will also cut back on commuting time. If you want to work with the elderly, call local nursing homes and ask what agencies they work with. Ask if they have a volunteer program. If you love animals, call a few veterinarians in your community and ask what opportunities might exist. Check out bulletin boards in grocery stores, gyms, and so on.

The local public library is also a great resource for finding groups in your area (they may want you too!). There are usually directories of nonprofit and social-service organizations. If you want to work in your community's school system, call the nearest school or the superintendent's office. Tell them that you are interested in helping out. Any religious organization (whether you belong or not) is another source of agencies in your area.

There are also local hospitals, museums, historical societies, and so on to investigate. Are there subjects in the news that you always keep up with? Are there situations that you feel are unjust? Do you have a desire to know more about something? Whether it's cardiac care or modern art doesn't matter. Follow your heart.

It Is OK to Ask Questions

Take the time to talk with several groups that interest you. Many organizations that depend on volunteer workers have orientation sessions which will outline the group's goals as well as discuss the opportunities for service within the group. If your chosen organization doesn't have such a program, make an appointment with the volunteer coordinator to learn more about what they do and who they need. Some suggested questions for a group are:

1. How is the group funded? This is important to people who want to know the political, corporate, or individual backing of an organization.

2. What is the structure of the organization? What is the ratio of paid workers to volunteers? How much red tape is involved in doing the work?

3. What does the organization expect of its volunteers? What are the responsibilities? Is there more experienced help available, or will you be all alone in your work?

4. Do they have a training program? These programs are a great

way to meet other new volunteers as well as learn specifics about your job. Be wary of too much responsibility with little or no training.

5. Are volunteers covered by the group's liability insurance policy? Depending upon the work you do, this is an important matter to discuss.

6. What are the goals of the organization? Make sure that the long-term goals of the institution are in harmony with your own desires.

There is nothing wrong with investigating a group before deciding to give it your time and energy. Doing your homework will help you feel good about your decision. It will also give you a chance to see if the chemistry is right. Do you feel comfortable with the surroundings? Are you compatible with the people you meet? Is the energy level of the group compatible with yours?

Making a Commitment

The best advice on making a commitment comes from Kenneth Dayton, longtime chairman and CEO of the Dayton Hudson Corporation:

> I think the important thing is for people to decide what they are really interested in, where they can make their contribution, and just let those organizations know. If they do that, they'll find that they will be asked. I pick the organization that I would most like to help and go to someone on that board and say "I'm very interested in what you're doing. How could I be helpful?" They'll find all kinds of ways for you to be helpful.

Most of us might not choose to go to a member of the board of directors, but we would be comfortable making a phone call and saying to the person answering, "Hello, I'm Jane Doe and I'm interested in doing volunteer work with your organization. Can you please connect me with the person I should talk to." The more thought you have put into what you want and can offer, the easier it will be for you to talk with the next person. The key here is to make the first call.

Be sure to talk with your family about your plans. It is important that those closest to you understand why you want to make a commitment to an outside group. You may find that your children or spouse want to get involved too. You can look together or encourage them to find an organization that works for them. Besides the walk-a-thons, there are many ways for parents and children to work together. Groups that work to improve housing often involve families. The Special Olympics also encourages family involvement. Scouting and becoming involved in school or after-school sports teams or clubs can combine volunteerism with family time.

Being a New Volunteer

We've already discussed the wisdom in starting slowly. Remember that added hours or responsibilities will almost always be available. Take the time to get comfortable and know your surroundings before committing to more than you know you can handle. Other tips for new volunteers are:

1. *Keep an open mind.* As with any new situation, it's important to listen before you decide what needs to be changed. People want to work with those who help solve problems, not those who *are* problems.

2. *Get to know your colleagues.* You've already got something in common with other volunteers—you care about the same issue. Talk with those who do the same or similar job as yours and learn from their experience.

3. *Be on time and reliable.* Many organizations know that some volunteers are less professional than others. Don't take the attitude that since you are not being paid, your professionalism is less important. Prove to the new group that you mean what you say. As with any job, the quality of your work will become known and your talents will then be sought out.

If There Is a Problem

All the research in the world may not prevent you from getting involved in something that isn't right for you. Sometimes it is the job itself; at other times it can be difficulties with a co-worker. And sometimes, with the best intentions, we may bite off more than we can chew. If there is a problem, and it can't be solved by a talk with a colleague or more experienced volunteer, discuss it with the person who hired you. Be specific. If you don't like the work you have been assigned, say so. There may be other opportunities that you would prefer. If nothing can be worked out, leave gracefully. That means that you give some notice that you will not be returning. Don't just stop showing up. Don't be discouraged. You are probably much better equipped to interview for a volunteer job than you were a few months ago. Keep trying until you find the place that's exactly right for you.

Moving Inward, Not Upward

Many people feel that volunteer work does pay, but that instead of money they are paid in a spiritual or psychic currency. Working in areas where the need for your skills and time is evident often provides a sense of satisfaction and worthiness that is not obtainable in other work arenas.

There's a saying from the early '90s that goes "You can't hug a BMW." Few of us have a BMW to think about hugging, but most of us do understand that there are times when our material needs and desires have been met, only to have a sense of being let down. There are days when looking in the mirror has nothing to do with toned stomachs or gray hair. Who is that person? Where did the time go? What have I done to leave my mark on the world? Volunteer work may not keep those questions from occurring, but it may well lessen the severity and frequency of their appearance.

The satisfaction of seeing your efforts pay off for other people is one of the richest rewards a person can have. To learn more about volunteer opportunities—from worker bee to sitting on the board

—read *Beyond Success: How Volunteer Service Can Help You Begin Making a Life Instead of Just a Living,* by John Raynolds and Eleanor Raynolds.

Things to Remember About Volunteer Service

- Through working with people and groups that need you, you may find deeper meaning in your life.
- This sharing of yourself can and should be from your heart, not your head.
- Volunteer work need not take advantage of the same skills that earn your living.
- It's important to take some time in deciding how and where you want to give your time.
- There are many ways for parents and children to work together.
- Keep trying until you find the place that's exactly right for you.

In Conclusion

Women in the 1990s are pursuing the kind of success they can't dress for—a balance of work, family, love and relaxation. At the same time, they are trying to cope with the care of aging parents, young children, careers, mid-life malaise and pressured marriages.

Studies show that American women find their own families to be the most satisfying parts of their lives, but that it's harder to be a parent "than it used to be." Difficult economic times have only added to the stress of "balancing it all."

All of us feel intensely the stresses of life in the '90s, but, also the satisfaction. We hope that *Balancing Acts!* has shown you how to bring your life into harmony and proportion by providing workable strategies.

We want you to enjoy all aspects of your life—at work, at home, with your family, with your friends. As we said in an earlier chapter, this isn't a dress rehearsal, it's the real thing. And it goes by so fast! We believe in you! Good luck!